CON

SOMERSET

Edited by Allison Dowse

To Freddie

Best wishes

from
James Webb

First published in Great Britain in 1999 by
YOUNG WRITERS
Remus House,
Coltsfoot Drive,
Woodston,
Peterborough, PE2 9JX
Telephone (01733) 890066

HB ISBN 0 75431 542 8
SB ISBN 0 75431 543 6

FOREWORD

Young Writers have produced poetry books in conjunction with schools for over eight years; providing a platform for talented young people to shine. This year, the Celebration 2000 collection of regional anthologies were developed with the millennium in mind.

With the nation taking stock of how far we have come, and reflecting on what we want to achieve in the future, our anthologies give a vivid insight into the thoughts and experiences of the younger generation.

We were once again impressed with the quality and attention to detail of every entry received and hope you will enjoy the poems we have decided to feature in *Celebration 2000 Somerset* for many years to come.

Longvernal Primary School

Melissa Light	64
Jessica Pole	65
Ryan James	65
Katie Smart	66
Holly Tetlow	66
Stacey Ryder	67
Chantel Kosmala	67
Gemma Sholl	68
Amy Vowles	68
Andrew Barnfield	69
Michaela Harris	69

North Newton CP School

Nicholas Tinsley	70
Dario Pickin	70
Tim Norman	71
Ben Sellick	71
Gemma Hogg	72
Daniel Duddridge	72
Elena Sharratt	73
Sophie Carney	74
Georgie Perry	74
Holly Pringle	75
Nicola Hesketh	75
Megan Goldie	76

St Louis School

Bryony Travers	77
Melanie Hardy-Phillips	78
Helena Enock	78
Zoe Marchment	79
Daniella Case	79
Tom Bradley	80
Alexander Bruce	80

Georgina Anstis	81
Thomas Harrison	81
Jordan Blake	82
Simon Latchem	82
Alice Asbury	83
Nicola Ewart	83
Jasmin Seymour Norris	84
Joanna Davis	84
Ben Lewis	84
Lesley Ann Payne	85
Joe Chedburn	85
David Bomani	85
Hannah Glynn	86

St John's RC Primary School, Bath

Clara Grant	86
Sophie Clesham	87
James Coram	87
Kerrin Rowland	88
Olivia Wiltshire	88
Oliver Bevan	89
James Barron	89
Soyntea Mead	90
Karlie Ayres	90
Emily Baker	91
Felicity Perkins	91
Tristan Kalsi	92
Sam Stratton	92
Thomas Barrett	93
Emily Brooks	93
Daniel Ryan-Lowes	94
Natalie Creevy	94
Lydia Saywell	95
Victoria Clifford-Sanghad	95
Hannah Newman	96
Gabriella Brand	96

Zoe Wrigley	97
Jonathan Horsfall	97
Declan Stewart	98
Kate Ealey	98
Chloe Watson	99
Christopher Ballans	99
Joe Locke	100
John-Paul Indoe	100
Tom DeMichele	101
Kieren Davies	101
Louisa Prentice	102
Sinead Rowland	102
Jolene Hartrey	103
Rebecca Morgan	103
Rosaline Dolton	104
Liam McSherry	104
Charles Perry	105
Kyle Stone	105
Charlotte Moon	106
Chloe Ridley	106
Adam Kingston	107
Samuel Crook	108
Alexander Johnson	108
Hannah Piekarski	109
Olivia Cundy	109
William Butler	110
Danielle Bolton	110
Joe Shannon	111
Liam Perdicchia	111
Hazel Walker	111
James Ellis	111
Liam Hopkinson	112
Alana King	112
Lisa Advani	113
Theodore Alexander	113
Virginia Golf	114

The Poems

SNOWFLAKES

Snow, snow f
         a
       l
        l
         i
          n
            g down
Making such a lovely sound.
We can make such big snowmen,
But if it breaks we'll start again.
Snow, snow is so white,
It makes a very lovely sight.

Matthew Delaney (6)
All Saints CE Primary School

SNOWBALLS

Snowballs on the window
Snow is everywhere!
On the roof, on the door,
It's everywhere, it's on your car.
Oh no! What are we going to do?
It's everywhere!
I don't like it!
What am I going to do?
Oh no! What am I –
A snowman. *Ahh!*

Jessica Gibson (8)
All Saints CE Primary School

THE LIFE OF A TIGER

The tiger smelling the fresh air in the cage at the zoo.
He thinks about the jungle with the trees.
He tries to escape, every day he sees the bluebirds and blackbirds
                                                    in the sky.
He's looking for his prey.

Edward Reid (7)
All Saints CE Primary School

SNOWFLAKES

Snowflakes falling down like feathers,
Snowflakes falling down so softly,
Snowflakes so white and light,
Snowflakes feel so cold,
Snowflakes move like the air,
Snowflakes sound like the wind.

Lorna Hinton (6)
All Saints CE Primary School

TIGERS

T is for tigers stalking through the long grass
I is for India where they live
G is for grabbing their prey
E is for extraordinary animals
R is for resting quietly in the sun
S is for save them, before they've all gone.

Jasmine Losasso (8)
All Saints CE Primary School

SNOWY NIGHTS

Gentle, soft, snowflakes
Falling down to the ground.
Feeling soft, falling ever so quietly.
Falling down, down, down, down,
Touching the ground with no sound.

Benjamin Tolhurst (6)
All Saints CE Primary School

SNOWFLAKES

It drifts like a feather,
We like to push it
and make snowmen and snowballs.
We make them in February.
We cook marshmallows on the fire
And cook roast pig.

Jack Webb (6)
All Saints CE Primary School

MY PUPPY

My pup's called Gizmo,
yelping when I step on his paw
playful
usually small and soft
peaceful when tired
pretty after bathtime
yawning before bed.

Melissa Nicholas (8)
All Saints CE Primary School

SNOWFLAKES

Snow, snow f
            a
              l
                l
                  i
                    n
                      g down,
twirling, twisting going to fall,
it goes on top of the wall.
We can make snowmen,
and have a snowball fight.

Arthur Riley (6)
All Saints CE Primary School

SNOWFLAKES

Every snowflake that falls down,
So calm and beautiful
As ever
Softly falling like a feather
So nice to see
What beautiful things they are.

Daisy Cooney (6)
All Saints CE Primary School

SNOWBALLS

Graceful, softly you can throw them.
You can play snowball fights with them.

Eve McWilliams (6)
All Saints CE Primary School

SNOWFLAKES

Snow, snow, falling down
Like a soft feather
Will you make a snow castle
Little snowflake?
Settling on the ground,
Make a snow street
With a fire to keep warm.
What warm tea are we going to have?
Play snowballs, do a snow fight
Watch a show?
Do you know I could eat snow,
Snow, snow, snow,
Snow, snow, snow.

Kieron Stephens (6)
All Saints CE Primary School

RABBITS

All day long rabbits
Hop
Jump
Run
Up and down hills
Their fur coats all covered with gold.
In the sunset they go down
Their big black holes
And then they are
                asleep.

Jessica Peterson (9)
All Saints CE Primary School

SNOWBALLS

Gently rolling up a ball,
Throwing snowballs at my friend,
White, thick and bright, it sounds
Like a frog jumping in the pond.
I like throwing snowballs,
They move fast, they are
White and bright,
It feels soft and cold.

Bethan Stevens (6)
All Saints CE Primary School

AUTUMN

King of the wind,
The leaves bend down,
The trees bow down.
When the King shouts
Twisting, turning and jumping,
The leaves must obey him.
And when the King is very cross
Everything bows down.

Joe Forward (10)
Calder House School

CHAMPION DOG OF THE WORLD

I'm the champion dog of the world,
I got on the roof and I hurled
A stone to the road
Where a croaking toad
Moaned, 'Oh, the champion dog of the world!'

Toby Coe (7)
Calder House School

HOLOCAUST

This was a happier place.
Oh yes!
But then Hitler cried
'You must be the blonde and blue eyed
And the Jews must die!'
'But why?' we cried
But Hitler had dying Jews reflected in his eyes.

The Jews were nothing but a wandering people
On a long and dusty road, with no hope,
Only a dream of one day,
That we would have a country
Like we used to have.

But now we must hide
From the marching boots
That hunt us down
To gas us.

Every day I think 'Why?'
When I see my friend and I know
That he's got one day left,
And I know I can't give my food away
Because my baby cries for it,
And it hurts when I know
My day of freedom may never come.

David Allen (11)
Calder House School

FIREWORKS ACROSTIC

F ireworks are beautiful things, well,
I think they are beautiful. Colours like
R ed, orange, yellow, purple - they just are
E xcellent. They go crash, bang,
W allop and my dog always barks,
O h, really loudly!
R ockets are the loudest and sometimes dangerous.
K ind people let them off
S afely so we don't get into trouble.

Benjamin Baker (8)
Calder House School

BLUE

Blue is like the sky
On a hot summer's day.
Blue is the sea on a calm night.
Blue tits come and land in my garden,
Blue is like dolphins swimming gracefully.
Blue is like the bluebells all along the field.
Blue is our school jumper
Warm as can be.
I like blue, don't you?

Edward Morgan (10)
Calder House School

RED

Red is blood,
Red is death.
Red burns,
Red kills.

Red covers soldiers
With terrible wounds,
Fractures, breaks.
Red gives aid.

Red is the nearest thing to hell.

Matthew North (11)
Calder House School

RED

Red is a fire, a blazing light,
Red is for an apple that grows on a tree,
Red is a fire engine rushing to its duty,
Red is for roses which you give,
Red is for a ball, which rolls and bounces around,
Red is for blood spurting out,
Red is for silk on a hat,
And red is my favourite colour.

Luke Harris (11)
Calder House School

AUTUMN

Damp autumn in the garden,
Crisp leaves fall from the trees.
A hedgehog assembles a nest in the hedge.
Squirrels hunt and hide their nuts
In secret places, deep in the trees.
But autumn to me is picking blackberries in the fields
And when I find conkers, so brown,
I feel really pleased.

Kate McNeil (10)
Calder House School

REFUGEE

Alone on the street, no more water
And I'm hungry and scared.
Nobody will give me food
Or water.
My feet are hurting.
Waiting for peace . . . so I can go home . . .
Go home . . .
Go home . . .
That's all I think of,
My small home
Not big,
Or wide
But a roof over my head.

Now I have nothing.
Too scared to go back,
Too scared to stay.
Getting soaking wet.
People stare at me,
People walk by
Taking no notice of me.

If you see me, please stop and help
A destitute refugee,
Please . . .

David Wells (12)
Calder House School

FORESTS AND WOODS

If you go to the forest,
With trees all leafy green,
Look closely,
Look closely,
You could see
A unicorn, snowy white with
A golden horn.

Forests and woods
Hold great secrets
My dear.

If you go into a wood
Look closely,
Look closely
You could see
A fairy fly with
Her silvery wings
And her silky hair flowing.

Forests and woods
Hold great secrets
My dear.

Leonora Fane-Saunders (10)
Calder House School

A 'THANK YOU' POEM

Thank you for making my clothes clean,
And looking after me when I'm feeling green.
I'm sorry for the times that I've been bad,
I hope I haven't made you mad!

David Yaun (9)
Calder House School

WHAT IN THE WORLD

What in the world goes
Jumping and trotting,
Eating hay and neighs?
What is it?

What in the world goes
Scrabbling and scratching
Looking for food
And goes to sleep in the autumn?

What in the world goes
Snuffle, snuffle, snuffle
And is very quiet?
Can you guess?

What in the world goes
Very, very slowly
And has a big shell?
What is it?

What in the world
Is very, very pink
And very, very fat?
Do you know?

What in the world goes
Bucking and jumping
If you stand in front of it?
What in the world is it?

Carly Stalker (10)
Calder House School

BLUE

The sky is a perfect blue,
High, high above me.
No clouds in sight.

The sea is a deep, clear blue,
Sparkling and splashing.
The dolphins dive deep
Through turquoise water.

Deep in the wood
Is a carpet of bluebells.
Blue is calm and gentle,
Feeling relaxed.

Blue is the perfect colour.

Huw Williams (11)
Calder House School

HAPPINESS

Happiness is no school ever,
Happiness is no girls,
Happiness is a sport's car,
Happiness is a chocolate world
Happiness is cricket all day,
Happiness is Christmas,
Happiness is teachers,
Happiness is a double ended water pistol,
Happiness is not money,
Happiness is life!

Nicholas Phillips (9)
Calder House School

THE WATERFALL

I am by the waterfall,
I can smell flowers
With the scent of honey.
I am watching the waterfall
And the trees are swishing and swirling
Backwards and forwards.
The water smells of raspberries,
And the soft heather has a sweet smell.
I am sitting by the waterfall
Smelling the flowers.

Victoria Singlehurst (10)
Calder House School

THE WIND

Wind, wind, wind, always blowing,
Always howling and helping.
Destroying, pushing, breaking tiles,
Irritating bees, blowing down walls,
Whistling, hurting injured people,
Chasing men, who can't stop it moving.
Flying kites,
Making some electricity,
Drying washing,
Sailing boats.
Sometimes wind is good.

Tristan Dunford (9)
Calder House School

A Secret Place

A secret place is where the sea is smooth
And gentle waves sway back and forth
To the rocks and beyond.
Where the seaweed slides
Across the glossy sand.

And you can sit by the sea,
Silence surrounds you
And you gather your thoughts
And fantasise your inner most feelings.

As night approaches the sky turns navy blue
And the stars begin to glisten.
The current dies down till
The waves lap gently on the shore.

As you look at the sea and the stars above
You feel calm and content.
Just lying there on the beach
In complete silence
In your secret place.

Corinna Wadsworth (12)
Calder House School

Bristol Acrostic

B usy Bristol on a
R ainy day. It is noisy and
I   t smells of car fumes,
S mells dirty.
T o me, it stinks.
O ften I cough loudly.
L ots of people cough.

Joshua Holland (10)
Calder House School

SPACE

I am in a spaceship
But I live down on the ground,
I listen and I listen,
But I cannot hear a sound!

I am in a spaceship
But I live down on the ground,
I often wonder what is down
So deep, deep underground.

William Harvey (9)
Hazlegrove School

THE INVALUABLE UFO

Once there was a creature,
A Mars Bar alien -
He lived in a broken down spaceship
Which was set up on Mars.
He lived with a friend and his brother
Who ate millions of bits of Mars,
While his friend made
Mercury trainers and autoboards.

Nicholas Crabtree (9)
Hazlegrove School

SPACE

Who was the first to land on the moon?
Who was the first to see a space balloon?
All these questions I ask myself,
All the answers are on my shelf!

Iain Farquhar (9)
Hazlegrove School

SPACE

A black, black hole in space,
Unknown things go on in space.
Aliens might be busy,
Making a ray,
A ray that could zap us!
A meteor might be on its way
To blow our planet up!

Marc Wakeham (8)
Hazlegrove School

HAPPINESS

Happiness is purple.
It tastes like melted chocolate.
It smells like flowers in the garden.
Happiness looks like a rainbow,
And sounds like singing birds.
Happiness is having a bath in melted chocolate.

Barnaby Redwood (10)
Hazlegrove School

ANGER

Anger is black,
It tastes like salt and pepper,
It smells like a piece of paper crackling in a fire,
Anger is a burning piece of carpet,
And sounds like gun fire.
Anger is boiling hot water, bubbling.

Harry Lauste (9)
Hazlegrove School

HAPPINESS

Happiness is yellow,
It tastes like melted gold.
It smells like a rose on a spring day
And looks like a lovely newborn puppy.
It sounds like a child playing
It feels like an open space where you
Can have fun and play.

Ben Hillier (10)
Hazlegrove School

SPACE

There was an alien bizarre,
Who lived on the North Planet R,
When a person attacked,
Who was called Iggozack,
He ended up with a scar!

Ben Mace (9)
Hazlegrove School

WORRY

Worry is blue.
It tastes like soggy fish and chips,
It smells of an old house,
It sounds like a cheering crowd gone silent.
It seems as though I should run away,
It feels as if my heart will burst.

Joshua Light (9)
Hazlegrove School

NO

No is a red word,
It smells like tomatoes
It's as hot as a fire,
As strong as a horse.
It's as mad as a hatter,
And as bad as a bear
No is as hairy as a spider.

Victoria Coates (11)
Hazlegrove School

WORRY

Worry is dark blue.
It tastes of hard sandwiches,
And smells of rotten perfume.
Worry looks like rain shattering down,
And sounds like howling wolves.
Worry feels very lonely.

Jack Byrne (10)
Hazlegrove School

THE WORLD

The world could be a wonderful place
If all we could do is live in peace
No wars, fighting, starvations or drought
Maybe one day, just maybe.

Ben Coles (11)
Hazlegrove School

THE HAG

The old tree wobbles early in the morning,
The old hag wakes as it is dawning.
The hag lies there dressed in black cloth
Nobody sees her face,
It is such a disgrace
Her cooking pot boils, then she uncoils.
On the other side, a fairy,
Who is not ugly or hairy,
Curls herself up as a petal of a flower.
The old hag's hair is rotten and sour,
At the end of the day
She coils up to say -
On Hallowe'en, on Hallowe'en.

Jack Bartholomew (10)
Hazlegrove School

THE LAZY WITCH

One windy night
When the moon was out,
A very old witch lay by a tree
Along came a fairy, who said
'What's wrong with you? Are you cold?'

The wind was blowing
Blowing so strong,
The witch had pointed toes
And a stabby nose.
'Go away, or I'll turn you into a toad!'

Emma Lloyd (8)
Hazlegrove School

SPACE

Up in space they had a race,
Well the planets did,
They did it in space.
At the race the stars sparkled,
And the moon gleamed,
It seemed peaceful
Until the race began!
Then there was cheering,
And the stars were peering,
Then the race ended.
The planet Saturn had won,
So the others hid,
Yes, they did.
They hid behind the moon,
But they will come out soon.
To orbit the sun once more.

Jessica Entwisle (9)
Hazlegrove School

THE LAZY WITCH

Wake up, wake up,
It is Hallowe'en!
There is much to be done!
There are toads to kill,
There are snakes to fry,
There are lizards to be gutted.
But the witch only cries 'Goodbye',
Goodbye, goodbye . . .
What sort of reply is that?
Oh wake up, wake up, please try!

Sophie Sweetman (10)
Hazlegrove School

MY MUM IS ALWAYS SAYING:

Tidy your bedroom!
Clean your teeth!
Make your bed!
Brush your hair!
Don't be late for school!
Finish your homework!
Get off the computer!
Go outside!
Get out of the bathroom!
Go and get my book!
Give me the newspaper!
Polish your shoes!
Have you finished your spellings?
Hurry up or you will be late for school!

Kit Lawson (10)
Hazlegrove School

A WITCH

There was an old witch,
Who had been shopping,
She bought shoes for her nose,
And clothes for her toes!
How much more confused could she get?

When she had bought,
Clothes for her toes and shoes for her nose,
She said 'I will get some money from the pet store,
And dog food from the bank - what a roar!'
So off she went for the pet food and money,
The shopkeepers thought she was crazy and funny!

Hannah Bearcroft (8)
Hazlegrove School

MUM SAYS

Mum always says get up
Or you'll be late for school!
Brush your teeth!
Get up you lazy girl!
Get your shoes on,
Hurry up!
See you later.

Turn the television off,
Go and read a book!
Go and play on the computer,
Time for tea!
Eat with your mouth closed!
Don't speak with a mouthful!
Go and brush your teeth!
Please go to bed!

Cornelia Turner-Klier (9)
Hazlegrove School

PATRICK O'HARE

Patrick O'Hare
was fond of a dare.
He would leap from a chair
or run around in his underwear.
He would not care
if he had to wrestle with a bear!
Yes, Patrick O'Hare
really lived for a dare.
Well . . . .
until he wrestled that bear
now . . . *gulp* . . . he's just air!

Sian Hewitt (10)
Hazlegrove School

SPACE

Space is a wild place
Where aliens muck about.
You will never be able to find a place like space,
I bet you will fly around without a doubt.

Spaceships are in space
Aliens are too.
Hop into a spaceship
And have a little zoom.

Sleeping upside down
You will find it rather hard.
Eating your breakfast on your side
Will be extremely hard!

If you ever go to space
You had better be aware,
There might be nasty aliens,
That will give you a little scare!

Chloe Anderson (8)
Hazlegrove School

WITCHY POO!

Witchy Poo! Witchy Poo!
I see you!
Don't hide from me,
Because I know where you are,
You're hiding in the bushes!
Hiding high and low,
Witchy Poo, Witchy Poo,
I see you!

Emma Oxenbridge (9)
Hazlegrove School

WITCHES AT A DANCE

The wicked witches, fly across the sky,
cross the sky and over the moon.
Far away to Witches Territory
Where they make potions strong.
Oil and boil,
A dead man's toe
A frog's leg,
A rat's tail,
Some bats' blood.
The tales of a witch
With a spiky broom.
Full of cobwebs, trees,
Bats, bugs and spells.

Thomas Tyley (8)
Hazlegrove School

THE THREE WITCHES

The three witches boiled children,
In the black bubbly cauldron.
Frogs' legs, rat's tongue,
Boiled while the witches sung -
Bibble, bubble, boil and trouble!

Bibble, bubble, boil and trouble,
The children were screaming,
And the witches' cats' eyes were gleaming.
The witches chewed on a tasty leg,
'What a tasty child!' they said.

James Webb (10)
Hazlegrove School

LAZY WITCH

Wake up Winny, it's Hallowe'en!
There's things to do and things to clean!
You lazy old witch, all sad and mean,
There's an owl on your hat,
Along with a black, furry bat!
A rat in your boot,
And a squirrel in the shoot!
Your broom is all muddy,
That's not going to be lucky!
You look like a spook
That is rather fluke!
Your cloak is in a tangle
Your fingers are old and mangled
Winny the witch, get up and stretch!

Simon Bourne (9)
Hazlegrove School

THERE WAS A LITTLE ASTRONAUT

There was a little astronaut
Who thought and thought and thought.
One day he was thinking
'I think the stars are twinkling'.
He swam back to his house on Pluto,
And started playing the fluto.
He sang a song, a jolly song
To make the stars shine brighter.
So the stars shone with zest,
People below thought it was the best
To watch from the Earth below.

Thomas Danaher (9)
Hazlegrove School

THE WITCH

Thin and ugly, clumsy like a dummy,
Riding on a broom in the skylight gloom.
Bang goes the broom; bang goes her hat
Falling down witch
Splat, splat, splat.
Into Witches Street so dirty, you can't see
Cans and rubber bands,
Ugly, don't you think?
What about her house?
All messy with nesting rats,
And cats and frogs and logs.
Thin as a pin,
Cold as a flood fold,
Blood flows from the sink into jars.
What will I find next?
This is jolly bizarre!

Hamish McLean (8)
Hazlegrove School

SPACE POEM

One dark night I decided to go to space,
So I got a rocket and went to space, oh space, oh space.
I passed the stars and the big round moon,
And spotted Mars and landed there soon.

It was very red and very hot,
So I soon turned into a cooking pot!
I began to shout,
But there was nobody about,
So I just stood and stared.

Constance Bennett (9)
Hazlegrove School

THE FIREPLACE

A mouth,
Blacker than coal,
Lies waiting.

A burning hot meal,
Glowing on a grey dish.
As it sucks the meal like spaghetti,
It breathes smoke,
Curling to the clouds.

But when it sleeps,
On a quiet summer's day,
It leaves remains of its food,
Grey as clouds on a dull day,
The fireplace waits.

Stephanie Bromage (11)
Hazlegrove School

THE VACUUM CLEANER

The vacuum cleaner is a dog,
Who has to suck up all the muck from the floor,
Then he gets stored under the stairs,
In his dark and dusty lair,
When the house gets dirty,
The dog comes out at six thirty,
And sniffs and snuffs around,
And makes a snorting sound,
The dog cleans up all the mess,
Then it gets put away,
For the rest of the day.

Albany Bell (11)
Hazlegrove School

A CLOUD

A cloud is a
Frosty balloon
Swallowed
Up by the sky
70,000 years ago.
Changing its temper every hour
It screams or shouts
When it's feeling bad
It beams and smiles,
When it's feeling glad
It cries and cries
When it's feeling sad
Though sometimes I wonder
As I look up at the sky
What is a cloud?
And the sky answers
Why . . .
A creation of God
With the love of me.

Layla Crabtree (10)
Hazlegrove School

HAPPINESS

Happiness is bright yellow.
It tastes like fizzy lemonade.
It smells like fresh roses.
Happiness looks like the sun, always so bright
And sounds like the gentle summer breeze.
It feels like being free.

Musab Khawaja (9)
Hazlegrove School

MY CLOCK

My clock is as colourful as a carrot,
All orange and bright.
As pink as a peach,
In the middle of the night.

But in the morning, it's as grey as a ghost,
During breakfast, it's as brown as toast.
At lunch time however it's changed to red,
As red as the Devil,
With fire on his head.

When night comes again,
It's as mad as a hatter,
It dances around,
It makes a big clatter.

Emma Hamnett (10)
Hazlegrove School

JULY

July is a colourful word,
That roams in my head,
As hot as Hawaii,
As playful as a pineapple,
As tropical as a tree,
And as sly as a snake.
As mischievous as monkeys can be,
As terrific as a tangerine,
As likeable as a lemon,
And as great as a grapefruit,
It tastes like a frozen strawberry freeze-pop,
Melting, just melting, very slowly.

Emily Horswell (11)
Hazlegrove School

WHEN I SLEEP

When I sleep, I do dream
The most horrific things.
There's sometimes grizzly monsters
Or slimy, slithery snakes.

Almost every time I dream
I am there.
I can't stand it when I die.
I either wake up in a fright
Or my dream goes fuzzy.

Then I go to a different place
I usually have some superb adventures.
Like the time I went back in time.
Then I wake up half asleep
'Just another dream,' I say.

James Atkinson (10)
Hazlegrove School

NOTHING TO DO?

Nothing to do?
Nothing to do?
Flush some jelly down the loo,
Fill your hair with nits and gnats,
Drive a car full of rats,
Put some worms inside Mum's bed,
Whack your sister till she's dead,
Tip everything out of the rubbish bin,
Prick your puppy with a pin,
Practise ballet in the kitchen,
Kick somebody like Miss Hitchen.

Rebecca Sainsot-Reynolds (9)
Hazlegrove School

DUSTBIN

Sits in the corner,
Waiting to be fed.
I watch it very carefully,
It doesn't move an inch.
My little pet monster
Eats anything it's given:
Leftovers, wrapping paper,
Anything's a treat.
Lunch time is its favourite,
There is plenty of food to eat.

When it's feeling full,
We empty it each night.
But it is soon full again,
Waiting for a meal.
We step on its foot,
It opens up its mouth.
We pop in the food,
And quickly rush away.
Then wait till tomorrow,
When a new day is here.

Nick Todd (10)
Hazlegrove School

MY PICTURE

My picture is as brave,
As brave as a lion
As sly as a fox
As clumsy as a ghost.

My picture is as sure,
As sure as a post
As great as a statue
As good as most.

My picture is as clever,
As clever as ever
As daft as a hedgehog
For ever and ever.

Rebecca Royle (11)
Hazlegrove School

ALSATIAN

The Alsatian is a mean, lean dog,
It hides in the shadows waiting . . .
For me!
I go past on my bike very carefully,
Then there's a growl getting,
Louder and louder!
I pick up speed,
With the dog right behind me,
I'm going downhill too fast, too fast,
Snap, my chain breaks!
With the dog right beside me,
I drop my bike and run!
I run past the sweet shop,
Past the pub,
Round the block.
There's my house,
I'm in the garden,
The dog's still there!
Through the door,
Lock the door,
Locked me in, the dog out,
I'm safe now . . .
Until tomorrow.

Adam Sheppard (9)
Hazlegrove School

NOTHING TO DO

Nothing to do?
Nothing to do?

Decorate your hand with glue,
Pour some sauce upon your head,
Make your enemies go red,
Saw your sister's swing in half,
Then smear some mud around the bath,
Roll your marbles down the stair,
And pull your sister's hair,
Hide the ice-cream far away,
Let the hamster out to play,
Open the door and let in Mum,
'You silly girl, there's lots to be done.'

Something to do!
Something to do!

Rebecca Barns-Graham (9)
Hazlegrove School

HAPPINESS

Happiness is yellow,
It tastes like toffee,
Hard and watery.
Happiness smells like horses' breath,
On a cold winter dawn,
Happiness looks like sunbeams,
Racing across a field.
It sounds like a nightingale
Singing sweetly.
It feels like the sun on your back,
Warming you through.

Emily Barran (10)
Hazlegrove School

FEAR

On a dark, dark night,
When all the stars were twinkling,
I was out in the tent,
My mum and brother were there,
Couldn't get to sleep,
I was twisting and turning,
I heard a noise,
Coming from the bushes,
'Arrghhh'
I screamed,
Mum didn't hear me,
I felt around,
Found a torch,
Switched it on,
And sitting on the grass . . .
Was a little tiny mouse.

Nicola Harris (10)
Hazlegrove School

THE HORRIBLE WITCH

The witch is pouring,
Frogs and dogs into the pot,
It is so very hot.
Witches live in ditches.

The witch is horrible,
Lamb and ham are thrown in,
She stirs and grins a grin,
Witches live in ditches.

Jennifer Holloway (8)
Hazlegrove School

NOTHING TO DO?

Nothing to do?
Nothing to do?
Flush your dog down the loo!
Sneak a hippo into school,
Push your dad into the pool!
Pull some paper so it tears,
Eat some really bouncy bears!
Make your great big pants explode,
Strangle a swearing toad!
Put lots and lots of ants,
Down your great big pants!
Sit on a tiny chair,
And eat your mop of hair!
Stick your tiny toes,
Up your great big nose!
Eat a massive stencil,
And a tiny pencil!
Make your head explode
Always talk in Morse code!
Eat lots of fire
Say 'Boo' to Kurtis John Dyer
Go fishing at eight
Use your sister as bait!
Turn on the tap
Now take a nap!

James Fausset (9)
Hazlegrove School

DARKNESS

Sent to fetch something from the bottom of the garden.
On the left's a terrace with several monsterish plants,
On the right's a field full of sheep,
A couple of foxes,
Dead sheep too.
Red monsters prowling
White ghosts howling.
Under foot there are thistles,
Green scorpion stings.
Ahead there's a tree,
Sixty feet high,
With prickly leaves,
Like Indian arrows.
Ahead still we have trees . . .
My den . . .
Dark and forbidding.
Some sheets of iron,
The corrugated stuff,
They make a shelter fit for three.
The hammer,
In the shelter;
Horrible and dark . . .
I go the lightest way,
Through the holly bush,
Sometimes the worst!

Tom Badham-Thornhill (10)
Hazlegrove School

MY DOG

My dog's as black as night,
She's a wonderful sight.
Her name is Ella,
But don't you dare tell 'er,
She'll go wild,
Just like a child.
She can smell a hare,
From anywhere!
She's got a habit,
Of chasing a rabbit.
Ella's the best,
Out of all the rest . . .

In the whole wide world!

Natasha Coates (10)
Hazlegrove School

THE MURDERER

She'll be there at the funeral
Solemn and sad
But underneath
She's really rather glad
She'll never be loud
She'll float there like a cloud
Over the morbid spectre
And as the mourners bend to pray
She gloats above the rector.

Harry Livingstone (11)
Hazlegrove School

THE GIRL I FANCY

The girl I fancy is a luscious sort.
With long, wavy hair, my friends say 'Cor'.
She walks down a path with a blue and yellow scarf
like a lioness hunting for prey.

She is rather nice. Tastes of sugar and spice
and she flies like a glorious dove.
She smells like roses and she poses to boys
who are coming her way.

I try to ignore her but I just have to store
the way she flirts with boys.
But I've got to say that on some days she
seems to flirt my way.

Daniel Lloyd (11)
Hazlegrove School

MANTRAP

A mantrap is like a vampire,
Waiting to bite the flesh.
Its teeth are like sharks' teeth,
Crushing, snapping every single bone.
It lies unseen under the grass,
Waiting for the victim to pass.
When the prey walks past
Snap
The hunter is satisfied at last.

Charlie Woollcombe-Adams (10)
Hazlegrove School

In The Morning

First I get out of bed,
Then I tease my sister.
'Leave me alone,' she shouts,
I try to irritate my brother.
'Go away,' he shouts,
'Mummy I ask . . . '
'Wait a minute,' she shouts.
'Daddy, can I . . .'
'Go away, I'm busy.'
So I get back into bed!

Millie Bacon (10)
Hazlegrove School

Prep

Prep is something nobody can bare,
It has been locked up for ages ready
To catch you, grasp you,
Children scribbling, staring, reading and whispering,
The teacher marking, working, chatting,
The bell rings and children file out
Shouting, skipping, running,
The prep room is silent, deserted, dead!

Isabel Lockhart Smith (10)
Hazlegrove School

Angry

Angry is a bad tempered lion
As fierce as fire
As red as blood
As spicy as curry
As howling as wind

Angry is a volcano erupting
As hot as July
As sharp as teeth
As poisonous as wild berries
As annoying as an anonymous letter.

Kate Flavell (10)
Hazlegrove School

SPRING LAMBS

All fluffy are little lambs,
Weighing fifty pounds
Some people think they're good on a plate,
But that's their fate.
They like to jump,
And are very plump,
Their wool is so soft
As they coughed
In the new spring air.

Lucy Pearson (11)
Hazlegrove School

THE MOON

The moon is a jellyfish,
Shimmering, silent and peaceful,
Watching over us,
Silver against the deep blue sky,
Mysterious, secretive,
Waiting till morning,
When she'll hide away,
Before the sun comes to chase her away.

Kim Gajraj (11)
Hazlegrove School

IT

It is a white word,
as blank as a white board,
as dumb as the roly-poly bird.
It is as stupid as a piece of paper,
as thick as wood.

It is as careless as a pair of shoes,
as clear as glass and
every time I use this word
careless comes into mind because
it is a vague word which doesn't explain itself.

Oliver Bendall (10)
Hazlegrove School

SPACESHIP

S paceships are zooming around
P lace to place, booming engines.
A liens are everywhere
C an anything happen?
E asy to be frightened and scared.
S parkling stars are so bright,
H anging around in the night sky,
I f only we could go to space
P laces unknown are exciting.

Carolyn Hignell (9)
Hazlegrove School

I FEEL SICK!

'I cannot go to school today,'
Said little Emma-Jane Mckay,
'Itchy spots! I have seventeen!
My face is going rather green,
I am too sick for chicken pie,
I'm going blind in my right eye,
I have just sprained my left leg,
I've shrunk to the size of a washing peg,
My heart has . . .
What was that you say?
Saturday? Saturday?
You say today is Saturday?
Goodbye I'm going out to play!'

Humphrey Gibbs (10)
Hazlegrove School

LONELINESS

Loneliness is a dry leaf amongst the meadow,
It is like a spooky spirit under the bedclothes,
The colour is grey,
It looks like the mid air at midnight,
And it smells like a dusty cobweb,
Loneliness feels like the way to dreaded hell,
It lives in the murky caves behind seaweed.

Flora Tolfree (10)
Hazlegrove School

THE WOOD

I am the wood,
The home of many different beasts,
I am big and dark and strong,
I thought no one could defeat me.

Some people came to chop me down,
My friends, the animals screeched and roared,
As their homes were crushed and ruined.

Now I am small, not half as big as I was
In those memorable days,
I have many companions, mostly birds,
Now a road runs through my trees
But I am still the wood.

Olivia Savage (10)
Hugh Sexey Middle School

THE STALLION

A gigantic beauty of a stallion,
fresh and responsive to my caresses,
head high in forehead
and wide between the ears,
limbs glossy and supple,
tail dusting the ground,
eyes well apart and full of sparkling wickedness
ears finely cut and flexibly moving.

Heather Ham (11)
Hugh Sexey Middle School

THE MARE

The sun dances gently on her
golden head. Her dark eyes like
ebony set in white gold, observed
her surroundings. Her beautiful
body glistened in tiny beads of sweat.

The scenery was a blur as he
raced towards her. She tilted
her head slightly as she sensed
his coming. She waited,
welcoming her young foal as he
drew near.
He was home.

Nicola Ham (11)
Hugh Sexey Middle School

FEAR

Your worst nightmare has just come true,
Fear is taking over you.
Shivering, shaking,
Time slows down,
Your head is spinning round and round.
Heart pounding loud and clear,
But all these symptoms belong to fear.
Your breath is there but you just can't catch it,
That knot in your stomach has got such a tight grip
The end of this must soon be here,
Why does it have to be so mean?
This thing called *fear*.

Laura Allison (10)
Hugh Sexey Middle School

The Millennium

Soon it will
be the millennium
and we'll be
able to watch
the new year appear
and bake cakes
while we stay
up late.
We'll be tired in the
morning and
my dad will
probably still be
snoring
and my sister will
be yawning, first
thing in the morning.
But I still can't wait
till the millennium
year appears
I just can't wait.

Tiffany Lane (9)
Hutton CE VC Primary School

Winter

In winter, snow falls from the sky,
and icicles hang from walls and drip.
It makes a puddle for me to jump in.
I'll go inside to get warm
and get all warmed up
and go back out again.

Aaron Page (8)
Hutton CE VC Primary School

THE STRANGE MILLENNIUM BUG

Does it have six heads,
Or does it have ten feet?
Does it eat cheese,
Or does it eat meat?
Is it orange,
Or is it blue?
Who does it look like,
Me or you?
Where did it come from,
Where will it go?
I wonder and wonder
But I don't know.
Does it sleep in a bed,
Or lie on a rug?
What is it?
It's the Millennium Bug.

Charlotte Walmsley (9)
Hutton CE VC Primary School

WINTER

Winter is freezing cold,
It has a lot of frost,
We play in the snow
And we throw snowballs
At each other
It is very cold, the snow
In winter.
We get presents at
Christmas.

Andrew Filer (8)
Hutton CE VC Primary School

MY CUDDLY LITTLE FRIENDS

There's a little brown mouse
in his tiny house,
his favourite food is cheese
and he doesn't like green peas.
He's really fast at running
and he's extremely cunning.
That's my little brown mouse.

I bought a new little bunny
and he loves it when it's sunny,
he's got a black twitchy nose,
whatever the weather it always shows.
That's my new little bunny.

Zoe Hoare-Matthews (8)
Hutton CE VC Primary School

SPRING

It's the beginning of spring
And new life begins,
There is Easter and
Chocolate and lots of things,
My birthday's in May
And I'm looking forward to that,
Plus there are lambs and ducklings
And lots of bees start
To come out and start to go *buzz*
And butterflies go *flap, flap, flap*
In the sun.

Keshia Heathman (8)
Hutton CE VC Primary School

IN SPRING

It's the first day of spring.
It's a bit misty, the children are happy.
Easter is soon, don't forget.
It's my friend's birthday, she loves spring.
Her favourite animal is a dove.
She loves the sky above,
it's a beautiful sight.

Daffodils come out, so do other plants.
The Easter eggs are hidden,
it's the middle of March,
it's nearly Easter.

Are you happy in spring?
I am.

Laura Heathcote (8)
Hutton CE VC Primary School

TIDYING MY ROOM

Every afternoon when I come home from school,
I have to tidy up my room because that's Mummy's rule.
I go into my room and shut the bedroom door,
I pick up all my toys and put them in the drawer.
I then go and pick up my shirt,
And in the corner I can see my skirt.
I gather up my socks, vest and tie,
And put them in the cupboard where they lie.
Then I put my foot on the ladder and start to climb,
It's nearly time for bed, so I shall have to end my rhyme.

Stephanie Carter (9)
Hutton CE VC Primary School

A Busy Day In A Hospital Ward

Nurses in, nurses out
Now and again you hear the doctors shout.

Mopping up and keeping busy
Often makes the patients dizzy.

Need a nurse, so ring the bell
How long you'll wait, only time will tell.

Feeling ill
And waiting for that pill.

2.30 is visiting time
And looking for that friend of mine.

The day goes slow
And back to bed, the routine I know.

Looking forward to another day
In the hospital bed I lay.

Maria Cox (9)
Hutton CE VC Primary School

In Winter

In winter, snow falls in the night.
The trees get sleepy, the clouds go grey.
Santa comes on Christmas Eve.

Winter is wicked,
and you go tobogganing down the hills.
December is just the best.

Grant Barwick (8)
Hutton CE VC Primary School

CENTRE PARCS

Centre Parc is so cool
When I jump into the pool
We can go on our bikes
And little children have trikes.

We can cycle down the lane
If you don't come, it's a shame.

There are bunnies
With fluffy tummies

That run around
Without a sound.

Best of all there are no cars
And at night, there's lots of stars.

Rachel Johnson (9)
Hutton CE VC Primary School

IN WINTER

Winter is cold
Winter is cold
Winter is cold
As cold as
Can be
And
Snowflakes
Fall
All around.

Philip Harris (8)
Hutton CE VC Primary School

SHHH

Get under the covers
Don't make a sound,
'Cause ghosts and spooks
Are all around.

In the hallway,
Near the chair,
By the bookcase
On the stair.
At first you may not
See them there.

But just lie still -

You will.

William Taylor (9)
Hutton CE VC Primary School

A WINTER'S DAY

On a winter's day
When the birds fly to warmer places
And the children play in the snow,
Trees have no leaves
And they sleep.
Clouds weep up all the snow.

In winter it is cold.
Snowflakes fall like
Sunflakes in the middle
Of December.

Alicia Patch (8)
Hutton CE VC Primary School

WHITE

White is a daisy in the sun,
White is a swan having fun,
White is a rabbit hopping around,
White is a Snow Queen in her snow gown.
White is the winter all around,
White is the pearl that has been found.

Kayla Harkins (8)
Hutton CE VC Primary School

THE LONELY STAR

The silent star shines down on me,
She glistens brightly for us all to see.
Her angelic light burns bright at night.
I gaze in wonder at the wonderful sight.
One day I will know the reason why,
I'm down here and you're in the sky.

Amy Parker (8)
Hutton CE VC Primary School

A WINTER'S DAY

Winter's cold, winter's freezing,
All the trees are covered in snow.
And I throw lots of snowballs until tomorrow.
January, February and December
Are all the months of winter.

Emily Dodd (9)
Hutton CE VC Primary School

MILLENNIUM

One thousand years since last we saw,
Such joyous moments enjoyed by all.
A long road travelled by many,
Both present and past.
Celebrate and be happy,
You saw in the millennium.

Chris Homer (9)
Hutton CE VC Primary School

WHITE

White is a cloud that floats in the sky,
You see it when it passes by.
It floats all day and all night,
High, high away.

It likes to be soft and gentle.
Dive through it and see.

Sophie Moment (8)
Hutton CE VC Primary School

WHITE

White is bright,
Just like a flashing light.
White is floating in the sky.
White is calm and soft,
Touch it if you can.
Jump up high and float on it,
Quick before you float through.

Harriet Osborne (9)
Hutton CE VC Primary School

WHITE

White is a pearl
In the deep, deep sea.
White is soft,
Feel it and see.
White is a cloud
Flying up in the air,
White is a daisy
In the sun.
White is a rabbit
Hopping around.
White is a polar bear
Running in the snow.

Stephanie Walker (8)
Hutton CE VC Primary School

SUMMER

Summer is hot,
Summer is sunny,
Children go to the beach.
Gentle breezes across the fields.
People go swimming.
Fruit grows on trees,
Flowers grow in fields,
Children go out to play.

Helectra Mahbouby (9)
Hutton CE VC Primary School

THE EXCITING YEAR

On New Year's Eve we can stay up late,
to wait for the exciting date
I felt I had to make a sign to say
goodbye to '99!
Millennium, millennium, at last it's here
the whole of the country will make a big cheer

Champagne and food, parties galore
and there's still plenty more

It's the end of the year and I still feel
like partying to celebrate the 2000 year!

Kirsty Ratcliffe (8)
Hutton CE VC Primary School

BLACK

Black is a misty night,
Black is a badger's hole.
As dark as a black panther,
As dark as coal.

Black is a puddle of ink,
Black is a horrible dream,
Black is a creeping mouse,
Black is a lady's scream.

Daniel Crosfield (9)
Hutton CE VC Primary School

A Zebra In A Zoo

He should be running free in Africa,
But poor zebra is stuck behind bars,
In a dark, concrete cell.

Zebra does not have any family,
Because a hunter came
To kill his family in Africa.
To get some money
For their skins of a magnificent pattern.
The hunter won.
He got the skins
And off he went to get his profit.

Zebra stares
At the crowd screaming and pushing
But what zebra hates most
Is flashing cameras day after day.

Zebra sulks a great deal because
He misses walking freely
In a wide space
Eating whenever he wants to
And eating different types of food.
Not just drinking water
And eating grass.

Zebra loves the end of the day
When everybody has gone home
Except the other poor animals
Locked up in their cells.

It reminds zebra
Of peace and quiet.
How life was
In Africa.

Kirstie Hellings (10)
Keinton Mandeville CP School

RED SKIN, BLACK SPOTS

Red skin
Black spots
Poisonous touch
Lily leaf he's poised on
Deadly in his leap mode
Sharp eyed as he looks around
The poisonous red arrow frog.

Watch him dart
Here and there
Like some kind of tribal dance, it seems
Big black eyes glance
Here and there
Brilliantly bright
Like stars.

Damp sometimes
Dry sometimes
In the jungle he creeps
On a lily leaf
He usually sits
Deadly, deadly,
Silent.

Be very careful,
Ah, don't touch
The little sweet thing
Is as deadly as a starving tiger
So don't take any chances
Pick up your things
And run!

Siobhân Viner (11)
Keinton Mandeville CP School

PONY IN THE STABLE

While I'm mucking out the stable,
I hear the clip-clopping of the horse's feet.
I'm walking the row of stables,
And come to my favourite pony.

Buttons, the Exmoor pony.

I peer over his door and stroke his soft neck,
His sweet innocent face like a new born baby.
His coat like a fluffy cat,
His pointed ears flicking with joy.

Buttons, the Exmoor pony.

I put down my equipment and lead him out,
His shiny grey coat stands out a mile.
I tie him up and put on
His shiny brown saddle and reins.

Buttons, the Exmoor pony.

Down in the riding school I jump upon him,
One small kick is all it takes till he's trotting.
When we've had our fun and it's getting dark,
It's back to the stable for my friend.

Buttons, the Exmoor pony.

I take off his saddle and reins for another day,
I put him in his stable with his supper.
I turn out the lights till tomorrow morning,
I can hear him munching, killing off his hunger.

Buttons, the Exmoor pony.

Amy Gornall (10)
Keinton Mandeville CP School

TIGERS

Stripes of black move all around me,
Vicious teeth are glaring towards my face.
Trees everywhere, surrounded with orange,
Where do I go? Nowhere to go.
Just move once and I'll be gone.
Quick pounces are made every so often towards me.
Quickly blood is scattered as a tiger jumps
And kills a small deer passing by.
Eyes staring straight ahead,
Paws dashing through the air
As more tigers join the group.
When, when will it be?
When will the first striped figure
Pounce towards me?
I need to run, but where to run.
There's no gap to run to safety.
Suddenly a large tiger,
Moves in its elegant ways towards me.
Nearer, nearer.
I have become a feast.

Hannah Jessett (11)
Keinton Mandeville CP School

A CHEETAH IN A CAGE

He sulks in the corners
Or paces up and down
He hides in the shadows
Or shows his growling frown.

But really he should be
In a golden grassy plain
Where the ground is boiling hot
And it hardly ever rains.

But he stares at the people
Who all stare at him
With their flashing cameras
That scare and frighten him.

But in his natural home
Whenever he gets near
A herd of stripy zebras
They all run in fear.

Holly Bryon-Staples (11)
Keinton Mandeville CP School

PANDA

Crunch, munch,
There goes another bunch.
I wish these humans would hurry up
And get some more bamboo.
Why can't these humans
Give me some more bamboo
And let me out of this cramped cage
Instead of goggling at me?
They just waste time.
They catch me
And then all they do
Is stare at me.
Can't people see
They are free.
But what about me?
I am not free
Though I wish I could be.
Yes, I wish I could be.

John Teague (11)
Keinton Mandeville CP School

GIRAFFE

It proudly strides with so much power,
Eating from every tree it finds,
Tortoiseshell patterns move quickly
Across the hot plain.
One kick from this beautiful creature
Will kill a lion.
It runs fast across the hot, hot plain,
Every now and then stopping
To look for danger.
In the distance you can hear
The light trot of its hooves.
Its long, long neck is
Tall and straight.
It can see for miles and miles
Always watching out for danger.
This beautiful creature isn't always
What is seems to be.
It may look delicate
But in the wild, it is not.

Katie Stace (10)
Keinton Mandeville CP School

A ZEBRA IN THE ZOO

He stands in the middle of the cage
Bowing his head, sulking miserably,
Waiting for someone to set him free
Back to his own home in the open wild.

As he turns his stripy head,
People say how lovely he is.
Waiting for someone to come and feed him,
He wishes he was in the wild eating his long grass.

People look through the rusty bars
With their flashing cameras,
Taking brilliant pictures of the stripy zebra
But he just really doesn't want to know.

Hannah Robinson (10)
Keinton Mandeville CP School

THE HUNTED

The fat brown rabbit keeps on running,
Behind him the huntsmen and hounds are coming!
As he runs he hears their cry,
And starts to think that he will die.
He jumps and hops, he thinks of the lake,
His life the huntsmen try to take.
He makes a dash, but then he stumbles,
And down a hill his body tumbles.
He hears the dogs, they bark and bark,
Everything begins to get pitch dark.
But up he springs, this desperate soul,
Those dogs would eat him up, and whole!
He tears across the long, damp grasses,
Which he tramples as he passes.
To the lake, he wants to go,
Running with his head down low.
He reaches his desired spot,
Breathing heavily, panting a lot.
He runs towards a hole in the ground,
Which he had previously found.
He leaps up high, but a dog snaps his jaws,
But trips and falls, head over paws.
The rabbit dives into his shelter,
The hunt was a real helter-skelter!

Michael Madelin (11)
Keinton Mandeville CP School

ELEPHANT

The elephant walks slowly,
Her grey trunk sways repeatedly,
Her tusks are white and shiny,
Her eyes are small as ping-pong balls.
Her ears flap loudly.
She is as large as a house.

Her baby stands lonely.
His eyes start to close.
His mum walks on quickly,
Or so it seemed to him.
He lies down carefully,
His tiny tail curls round him.

His mum walks back to him,
And lies down quietly,
By his side.
The last gold glimmer of sun goes down,
Slowly, slowly.

Sophie Constantine-Smith (11)
Keinton Mandeville CP School

WINTER TREES

Winter trees
Standing up straight
Like soldiers proud
Against a sapphire sky
Hands like skeletons
Reaching out for the stars.

Melissa Light (8)
Longvernal Primary School

THE MILLENNIUM

What will change by the year 2020?
Cars will fly, you'll see them fly by and by!
What else?
We'll have telewatches, you'll see aliens with red and yellow blotches!
Anything else?
We'll live in perspex houses and we'll live on planet forces!
Come on, tell me more.
A robot will do your schoolwork, one will do your homework!
You're not telling me something.
There'll be a 're-inventor', it'll give us an old time tour.
What else?
The world will never be the same again.

Jessica Pole (9)
Longvernal Primary School

WINTER TREES

As dark as space.
Frozen statues.
Stuck on a ruby background.
Arms reaching
For things.
As pointed as a cactus
Sitting on their own.
As colourful
As a ruby rainbow.
As red as a ruby.
As blue or purple as a sapphire ring.
As shadowy trees stand alone.

Ryan James (8)
Longvernal Primary School

THE MILLENNIUM

Lots of computers going wrong,
Big Ben doing a special dong.
The new century is quite near,
Thousands of people drinking beer.

People partying everywhere,
They're building the Dome with lots of care.
Pop songs coming out in the country,
Apples that taste much more munchie.

They're building better transport by air,
They've got no bolts to spare,
For the people building need all they've got,
Will they finish the Dome or not?

Katie Smart (10)
Longvernal Primary School

BONFIRE NIGHT

Rockets zooming,
Then they're booming,
Catherine wheels spinning,
Everyone's grinning.
Glittery sparklers, sparkling.

Fountains curling,
More Catherine wheels whirling,
Cracklers crackling,
And there's rattling.
Screamers screaming in the air,
'I don't want to go home, it's not fair!'

Holly Tetlow (9)
Longvernal Primary School

MILLENNIUM

The millennium is coming our way.
It will be really fun on the actual day.
With parties and speeches and very late nights,
I wonder if the millennium will be such a fright?

The last day of the world is coming
Our way, so they say, is it true?
Will it really be as bad as everybody thinks?
I don't know, do you?

I'm not sure about the millennium
What will people think? What will people say?
What will we play with?
What will we be?

Will TV change? Will our mums still make
The tea? I really, really hope it doesn't change too much.
I hope the Spice Girls stay, I hope they don't stop.
I hope we don't become robots or live in squats.

Stacey Ryder (11)
Longvernal Primary School

WINTER TREES

They are some soldiers in the scarlet sky
They are dark shadows against the sapphire sky
As the sun goes down
They are a bunch of wooden arms
Reaching for the stars.

Chantel Kosmala (8)
Longvernal Primary School

ABOUT THE MILLENNIUM

Computers going wrong
Big Ben going *dong*
New inventions
Building conventions.

The Dome will be fun
What else will be done
With new cash
There's going to be a dash.

I can't wait
I'm nearly late
There's Big Ben's chime
It's the year 2000.

Gemma Sholl (10)
Longvernal Primary School

WINTER TREES

Frozen skeletons,
grabbing hands,
all silhouetted
against a sapphire
and scarlet, dusky sky.

Amy Vowles (8)
Longvernal Primary School

THE YEAR 2020

In the year 2020 you will do homework on a computer.
What else?
You will contact your friends on a watch.
What else?
Robots will do the housework.
What else?
We will have inflatable houses.
What else?
We will have multicoloured computers.
What else?

Andrew Barnfield (9)
Longvernal Primary School

FIREWORKS

Crackling, zooming, swirling, whizzing.
Oh my ears! What is that twirling?
Screaming rockets, it's getting quieter . . .
Oh no, here it starts again . . .
Zapping, swirling, booming,
Pinks, purples, sizzling, crackling,
Bang! Bang! Help, I don't like fireworks!
Greens and blues spitting.
Fizzing, rattling, booming, sparkling, spraying.
Suddenly it ends, no more noises.

Michaela Harris (9)
Longvernal Primary School

BUGS' BALL

Wriggling worms dressing in brown.
Crawling centipedes going to town.
Beautiful butterflies dressed to kill.
Moaning millipedes eating their fill.
Spooky spiders spinning webs.
Baby beetles in their beds.
Dancing damsels twirling round.
Grasshopper group what a sound.
Flighty flies dancing late.
Miserable maggots with their mates.
Water boatman skimming around.
Sleepy slugs lie on the ground.
A jolly night enjoyed by all.
Everyone was at the ball.

Nicholas Tinsley (9)
North Newton CP School

THE TIGER

T he mighty tiger
H e moves with such speed.
E veryone fears him.

T he speed of him, but
I   can see him
G oing through the undergrowth
E ars that hear everything
R oaming through the jungle.

Dario Pickin (9)
North Newton CP School

CELEBRATION

C elebration
E njoy a big celebration.
L et your joy flow out, to the heart.
E at the food at the big celebration
B urn the sobbing and make happiness
R affle tickets being won.
A t the celebration there are presents,
T ake the presents (but only if you won)
I t would be a shame if you burst the balloons.
O ops I've done it
N ever mind I'll fix it later.

Tim Norman (8)
North Newton CP School

CELEBRATION - THE WORLD CUP

People shouting rattles rattling,
Excitement in the air,
At last it is the happy day,
Colour everywhere,
I have got my tickets,
I hope my seat is good,
I have got my scarf and hat,
And a rucksack full of food.

Ben Sellick (8)
North Newton CP School

FIREWORK, BONFIRE AND ME

Lovely firework would you please tell me why
you glow just for me?
A little less dazzling please, please, please.
Do it a little less dazzling
oh do it for me.
I've only just started oh no, no.
I'll go a little brighter.
Oh ho, ho,
dazzling rain, dazzling stars
flying saucers
oh hurrah,
diddle de diddle do I've got a surprise
waiting for you,
a bonfire just for you
such crackling, such brightness
crickle, crackle, crickle cre
do it a little less bright
just for me.
I've only just started
crickle, crick, cre.
I'll make it brighter
just for me.

Gemma Hogg (9)
North Newton CP School

WHEN I WENT FISHING

As I felt a bite on my line
a shiver went down my spine.

As I went to get the landing net
I fell in and got terribly wet.

As I reeled in my line
I started to whine
but then I was fine.

As I went to get a glass of beer
I saw a fish that looked queer.

Daniel Duddridge (10)
North Newton CP School

THE SUN PRINCESS

Silvery, golden rays,
Shone down with fiery red blazes.
Raining showers of gold,
Trickled down with dazzling stars.
The sun princess had arrived.
She stepped out of the river of light.
Graceful and swift as a feather.
Her hair was no more
Than a golden mist.
The long shining pleats of her dress
Made me squint.
Her large golden crown, almost floating
Above her head.
Everything about her seemed magical.
There was a faint tinkling sound
As the sparkling stars fell down
From her lovely locks of hair,
Scattering on the ground.
Then her dancing voice cried out,
'May the sun shine on!'

Elena Sharratt (10)
North Newton CP School

CELEBRATION!

C elebration!
E aster eggs are for Easter,
L ight up your pumpkin and let it glow,
E veryone celebrates Guy Fawkes,
B oys and girls are being born,
R abbits, hens having chicks,
A t celebration time everyone's happy,
T elling stories to the children,
I play with my friends when we celebrate,
O pening presents is such fun on birthdays,
N oisy children celebrating every day!

Sophie Carney (9)
North Newton CP School

CELEBRATION

C arnival night all dark and bright.
E aster time has come again, chocolate eggs and a big fat hen.
L ively children come out to play, little creatures love the day.
E veryone loves Christmas day when presents have made their way.
B irth of Jesus is long away but we still celebrate the day./
R esurrection when Jesus comes back to life.
A dam and Eve were the first to celebrate life.
T he time has come to celebrate the day when Jesus was crucified.
I really like Easter with creamy chocolate eggs.
O n Christmas day we celebrate Jesus' birthday.
N ice food to celebrate.

Georgie Perry (9)
North Newton CP School

CELEBRATION

C elebration
E aster eggs
L ent
E ating chocolate
B ringing home present
R abbits having babies
A t celebration everyone has a party
T elling stories
I go and help my mum
O ther people laughing
N ice food.

Holly Pringle (9)
North Newton CP School

CELEBRATION

C ome on in it's time for celebration
E aster is here
L ent
E aster eggs
B onnets
R affle tickets
A fter Jesus was born
T own where Jesus was crucified
I n Jerusalem
O pening Easter eggs
N ow it's time to celebrate.

Nicola Hesketh (10)
North Newton CP School

FIREWORKS

Red and orange fire leaping
up into the sky,
sparkling stars twinkle down
in a smoky mist.
Golden rays of light leaping up
illuminating the blackness.
Making a magical world shining down on the crowds,
their eyes squinting in the light.
Then it fell . . .
fading down to the ground,
slowly, slowly dying.
There was silence, it was deafening
everyone waiting for the boom.
It came louder than ever.
Children cover their ears,
trying to stop the ringing,
the everlasting noise,
craning over the heads of adults who
block their view.
But it's ended.
All finished.
Waiting to be born again
next year.

Megan Goldie (10)
North Newton CP School

MY SKIING HOLIDAY

Day 1 - I start skiing tomorrow (Monday),
Unfortunately we only stay till Sunday.
Flying all over the place, whoopee,
Sliding down on your bum, wee.
I've hired all my stuff from boots to skis,
They're so smelly they'll soon be attracting fleas.
I'm full from tea,
I want to ski.

Day 2 - A new day is dawning,
It all started in the morning.
We got off the ski bus,
Not making a great deal of fuss.
We started skiing, sorry let me rephrase that,
Falling over in the snow,
Goodness what a show.

Day 6 - Today's is Christmas Day,
Santa's been with his sleigh.
The presents were mounted so high,
That they reached the sky.
I had a sweetie kebab, it tasted fab.
Off to church we did go,
It was all in Italian and was rather slow.

Day 8 - We were on the leaving bus by 6.30,
Our friend was complaining that her leg was hurting.
It still did not snow,
But the bus had to go.
Even though my ski suit's all wet,
This will be a holiday I'll never forget.

Bryony Travers (11)
St Louis School

The Firework Display

You're waiting, waiting impatiently for those brightly coloured
fireworks to go off.
You're standing there in the cold,
unaware that they will whiz off any minute.
Screech, bang!
The amazing, brilliant colours fill the sky!
The first firework attracts everyone's attention.
All of a sudden five dazzling, fantastic, swirling Catherine wheels
all go up, up, higher into the dark sky all at once.
Rockets are shooting in all directions, banging at the very end.
Everyone is holding spitting, silver sparklers,
and waving them in the air.
Fountains and fountains of fireworks going off one after the other.
People are wearing gleaming, glow-in-the-dark necklaces.
It's a wonderful night.
The fireworks carry on zooming until very late,
when the displays finished we all go home to bed.

Melanie Hardy-Phillips (10)
St Louis School

Safari In Kenya

Safari in Kenya
really is brill,
maybe you should try it some day,
noisy elephants or
roaring lions
could keep you awake half the night,
but don't forget the king's who are the meanest,
but the cleanest are the leopards.

Helena Enock (10)
St Louis School

THE JUNGLE

The jungle is dark
The jungle is light
A lion will roar
And give you a fright!

Boo! Boo! Boo!

The jungle has day
The jungle has night
A tiger will roar
And give you a fright!

Boo! Boo! Boo!

Zoe Marchment (9)
St Louis School

THE WATERFALL

The waterfall is splashing, crashing and bashing,
The spray falls like mini diamonds and makes my hair all dewy.
It falls to the ground like a howling hound,
Just ready to bound off the rock.
A colourful rainbow scatters across the sky,
Making a reflection onto the water,
The rain is making the waterfall louder,
Thunder and splashing.
It hollows and echoes in the cave behind,
And it dies down as the rain stops,
And it gets quieter as I listen.

Daniella Case (10)
St Louis School

MAX MY CAT

Max my cat is a real wimp
He sleeps nearly all the time
On my bed, on the sofa
On top of the cupboard
Under the table
He doesn't care
He just curls up
Just goes to sleep purring
But at night I don't know what he does
He might fight
He might even sleep
It remains a mystery
What Max my cat does at night.

Tom Bradley (10)
St Louis School

BLUE

Blue is a turquoise stream with a dark dissection through the middle.
Blue is like a bleeding mountain with navy slicing through the centre.
Blue has cascades like a galloping, crashing wave.
Blue has an addiction to life, an amazingly, strong craze.
Blue is a whale with different shades of gold.
Blue is young, smart and bold.
Blue is like a myth, an unknown dream.
Blue is so stunning, it makes you want to scream.
Blue is like a bird soaring up in the sky.
Blue can either be gloss, wet or dry.
Blue is a wolf howling to the moon,
Blue is lost in a merciless typhoon.

Alexander Bruce (11)
St Louis School

SCHOOL

School, school, school
Some like it, some don't
School, school, school
Sometimes nice, sometimes not
School, school, school
Girls and boys
School, school, school
Teachers and pupils
School, school, school
Playtime, hooray
School, school, school
Oh no more work
School, school, school
Yes Miss
School, school, school
Home time, yippee!

Georgina Anstis (8)
St Louis School

SCRAMBLING

The gun fires and the bikes are off,
The howling, crashing, roaring sound of the engines,
The scramblers go rolling, crashing and smashing down the steep,
                                                    rocky hills,
Eight of the twelve bikes are still racing,
Number seven is going to win,
Number eight is catching up,
But seven has gone skidding past the line first,
He has beaten all the other bikes.

Thomas Harrison (10)
St Louis School

DINO ASSASSINATION

The raptors sight prey,
A big, juicy Iguanodon,
The raptors round it up,
The sound of angry roars,
Feet clattering and booming,
Screeches and roars,
Bangs and booms,
Claws thrashing and lashing,
The raptors assassinate,
Murder, rip, sacrifice, claw,
The poor Iguanodon breathes
Its last breath.

Jordan Blake (10)
St Louis School

SHADOWS

Shadows are dark and they have no friends,
Its enemy is light,
It creeps up on anything smaller than itself,
Growing bigger and bigger and bigger!
It follows you copying your every move;
It does not speak, it does not make a noise,
Shadows can learn as they work out your weakness,
The shadows use your imagination,
It moans and groans coming from the stairs,
The kitchen lights buzzes and the shadows disappears,
I am safe I was sleep walking.

Simon Latchem (11)
St Louis School

THE CAT

The tubby, tabby tortoiseshell
Around the fire in a curl,
But suddenly he leaps at you,
He seems to screech and scratch and mew.
Thinking he has done some good,
He races off to find some food.
But he says 'That's not quite enough,'
And then runs off to find more stuff.
He prowls and yowls for quite some time,
And then, when he has had his dine,
For an hour or more he hunts and roams,
Until he goes right back the whole way home.

Alice Asbury (10)
St Louis School

THE STORM

The storm crashes and the rain lashes down,
the thunder groans, moans and feels like a great giant is going to
stamp on you with its huge thumping feet.
You get into bed, suddenly there's a crash of lightning,
it strikes in the sky.
You suddenly dive under your covers trying not to be scared.
The storm is like a huge, metal ball going to come thundering down.
Then the wind starts howling,
and you can hear the dustbin toppling, falling over.
Then the storm calms down and suddenly stops,
everything goes quiet and I slowly fall to sleep happily.

Nicola Ewart (10)
St Louis School

AUTUMN

Autumn is a time when all the leaves start to fall off the trees.
Then the wind starts to blow really hard.
In autumn you see lots of people out with scarves,
hats and gloves on.
Nobody really wants to go out now.
When you're tucked up in bed, you will feel warm with your
pyjamas on.
The leaves go all crunchy and brown underneath your shoes.
Now go to sleep tomorrow, hopefully, will be a warmer day.

Jasmin Seymour Norris (10)
St Louis School

THE HUNTER

The eagle flies swiftly above all the bright, green trees
The silence of the forest gives the hunter a good chance
The hunter glides, drifts, floats, slides and skims
All the little creatures shiver, tremble, shake and quivers
Until the hunter flies in a different direction
Squirrels scamper, scuttle, zoom and run up and down trees
The hunter aims, attempts, intends and endeavours but misses his prey.

Joanna Davis (10)
St Louis School

WHALE

The whale thunders through the crashing, roaring water
When the whale is chasing the shoal of fish
Zooming through the clashing of the waves
The fish dart, sprint through the splendid, sparkling ocean
The whales swiftly, sneakily catch their prey.

Ben Lewis (10)
St Louis School

HANDS

Hands are the tools of an artist
To paint the world at large
To shape the emerald trees
To fold the sapphire seas
The touch of life to a blank canvas
Hands create the image, the dream
Hands are the flowing life
To add detail
Hands can paint life and life itself.

Lesley Ann Payne (11)
St Louis School

THE DARKNESS

The darkness is a black hole and seems just like space
but with no stars.
It's just like being inside a dragon's stomach.
It's like being all the way down at the bottom of the ocean,
all dark and gloomy.
Darkness is scary.

Joe Chedburn (11)
St Louis School

GOLDEN

G lowing sunset in late afternoon
O n the sun the heat lies
L iving there is a place to hide
D estination has arrived
E vil things come out at night while the sun is not alight
N othing is better when the sun is light.

David Bomani (10)
St Louis School

THE ZEBRA

The zebra drinks from the waterhole
Some stripes as white as snow, some as black as coal
A tiger comes looking for its prey
Through the mud as thick as clay
The tiger pounces for its meat
The zebras see him before he eats
The tiger sprints off, he knows he's beat
He has to take it, he's had a defeat.

Hannah Glynn (10)
St Louis School

HOW WE WERE

Screaming and crying
That's how my life started
First day of school
And the Christmas play
My birthday cake
My first Easter egg
My second teddy bear
'Bye bye darling, have a nice day and work'
My first book
My first test
Sandcastles
My nose and cheeks full of cream!
How we were
Just look at me now!
Grey hair and wrinkles everywhere
How we were
Spots and greasy hair
How we were.

Clara Grant (10)
St John's RC Primary School, Bath

THE EARTH

The earth trembles and shakes
When people kill animals and don't look after the earth
Otherwise gone forever.

The earth trembles and shakes
After pollution takes over and kills everything
Animals and people are dying because of factory smoke.

The earth trembles and shakes
When the people take animals and homes
away from the rainforest
Now see what we have done!

Sophie Clesham (9)
St John's RC Primary School, Bath

POLLUTION

Pollution, pollution
smoking up the street
Pollution, pollution
swirling around my feet

It poisons the river
That makes me shiver
It pollutes the air
That's not fair!

I sometimes think
Why did they make cars?

James Coram (9)
St John's RC Primary School, Bath

CHANGES

One year to go, one year to go,
I wonder what might change?
Food, houses or people,
Or animals, clothes and hair?
Will pollution stop?
Will the whole world change?
Will extinction stop growing?
Who knows?
How time flies, oh how time flies!
Will this year go by quicker?
Will robots do our housework,
Or will doctors have robots for staff?
What a celebration it will be that day,
With champagne, fireworks and games.
I can't wait any longer,
I'm going to go mad!
But that'll be the day,
When the whole world will change!

Kerrin Rowland (10)
St John's RC Primary School, Bath

THERE'S NOTHING NICER THAN...

There's nothing nicer than sweets and ice-cream.
There's nothing nicer than dreaming wonderful dreams.
There's nothing nicer than hot garlicky lasagne.
There's nothing nicer than firm ripe bananas.
There's nothing nicer than hot bubble baths.
There's nothing nicer than having a good laugh.
There's nothing nicer than having good friends.
And this is where my poem ends.

Olivia Wiltshire (8)
St John's RC Primary School, Bath

INVASION OF THE SNAKES

Streaking through the bushes,
One giant rush of colour in the rainforest,
An army of snakes,
Rushing towards the African village,
The residents don't know they're coming,
No people expect them.

People hear rustling through the bushes,
They know what it is and run for their lives,
And on come the snakes,
Spreading themselves all over the village,
Spilling all over the village,
Killing every living thing.

They eat their way through everything,
Everything is at risk,
All the snakes looking like a carpet of maggots on the floor,
Spitting, killing, eating, squeaking,
People are dying,
All things are alive.

Oliver Bevan (9)
St John's RC Primary School, Bath

MY FRIENDS

I have a cat who is much too fat
I have a dog who sleeps like a log
I have a mouse who lives in my house
I have a fish who eats off a dish
I have a snake who's never awake
These are my friends for whom I care
Come and visit if you dare.

James Barron (9)
St John's RC Primary School, Bath

FOG

Slowly the fog comes
round and round
the corner
to a town
past the houses
and a school
he makes his way
to the field
to the old farm
where he lived a very long time ago
he woke with his shoulders
crunched
up and head down.

Soyntea Mead (9)
St John's RC Primary School, Bath

SPRINGTIME

This morning I woke up warm in my bed,
It's spring, it's spring,' I said.
It's strange I'm sure the garden seemed so dead,
All brown and mushy, no signs of yellow or reds.
Now all I see is great flower heads,
Look, just look at that flower growing with all its power!

Look at that bird perched on my slide,
Singing and dancing with all his pride.
I think it's a thrush looking at the girls
and making them blush.
Oh how I love springtime.

Karlie Ayres (9)
St John's RC Primary School, Bath

WISHES AND DREAMS

Sitting on a water lily in the yucky, smelly pond,
Waiting for my chance,
My lovely dream,
I'm bored of splashing about in gunk,
Looking at other ugly frogs,
I always miss my chance,
When she has rowing lessons,
But then again,
I didn't miss one chance,
I saw her soft fair face,
Her long flowing hair,
But she kissed the wrong frog!
She hasn't come down since then,
It was said she was horribly ill,
So I am now stuck,
Forever?

Emily Baker (9)
St John's RC Primary School, Bath

THE SUN

The sun is very light
And beams down on me
I get very hot
I love it a lot

The sun's bright light
Shines in the day
It makes flowers grow
And I shout hooray, hooray, hooray!

Felicity Perkins (9)
St John's RC Primary School, Bath

THE WOODS AT NIGHT

The moon shines down on me,
Leading a trail into darkness.
A chill runs down my spine,
As thorns scratch my neck.
A soft rustling noise echoes
Through the woods as I walk
Over a sea of leaves.
The owl sits on his branch and
Hoots an eerie noise into my ear.
Continuously, and the rabbit burrows
Down into his hole to escape a predator.
The sky seems to watch me,
An endless path into a odd world.

Tristan Kalsi (10)
St John's RC Primary School, Bath

THE YEAR 2000

There's lots of mayhem, lots of madness.
Do you know why?
Because of the millennium.
Everyone's going crazy, booking holidays
and having parties all night.
Some people are even going to have a great time on the other side
of the world.
In New Zealand it's the first place sun's glittering rays
jump like a kangaroo onto mountains and grass of New Zealand.
Oh yes and I forgot to tell you,
I'm going too, so come and join the madness,
it's going to go off with a bang.

Sam Stratton (10)
St John's RC Primary School, Bath

THE DARK MIST

As the wind blows it wraps around me,
Am I floating?
No, but I feel the wet grass beneath me,
Then I hear a sound,
A 'whistle', a 'shhhhh' and a 'hiss',
Now it's crawling up my body,
It's nearly at my head!
Now I'm lost, stuck in this illusion,
'Help!' I shout as I fall to the ground,
Now it's crawling into my mouth!
It's out now leaving a taste of coal,
Now as I lie still my body turns to ice,
Now it clears, it's grey-white and black,
As it goes it leaves a thick black trail,
Now I'm safe in the moonlight.

Thomas Barrett (10)
St John's RC Primary School, Bath

FOG

The fog is thick
Thick, thick
The dark garden full of fog
Comes up from the sea and spoils the earth
The sea has a black face
When it's ready it comes out and darkens the earth
I stand in the middle of the dark earth
Waiting, waiting silently waiting for it to disappear
Waiting for the sun
Waiting for the new millennium?

Emily Brooks (9)
St John's RC Primary School, Bath

TIME

Time is everywhere,
Hours, minutes, seconds,
Tick tock, tick tock, tick tock,
1066 Battle of Hastings,
Tick tock, tick tock, tick,
1666 Great Fire of London,
Tick tock, tick tock,
1815 Lord Wellington at Waterloo,
Tick tock, tick,
1837 Queen Victoria
Tick tock,
1941 World War 1,
Tick,
1969 First spaceship on the moon,

Millennium,
For now, we turn a new page in history,
2000!

Daniel Ryan-Lowes (10)
St John's RC Primary School, Bath

NEW MORNING

The bright sun rises and here's a new day
The loud cockerel crows in the old fashioned way
The sun dial casts its shadow so dark
I hear in the garden the dog start to bark
The new, fresh dew smell whirls up my nose
I see out the window a new summer rose
This peace and tranquillity was always meant
To make people joyous, pleased and content.

Natalie Creevy (10)
St John's RC Primary School, Bath

THE ENVIRONMENT

I remember when we
looked after the environment
every day was a sunny day
the birds singing quietly in
the morning and children playing
in the street
but now just a dusty
road no birds singing and no
children playing no shining
sun glistening just dark clouds
all that brightens up the
night is the shining moon
and twinkling of the stars
every day the environment
is dying

Lydia Saywell (9)
St John's RC Primary School, Bath

WHY?

Why do people want his fur?
Why don't people care?
He wanders what the future will bring,
joy or pain?
He does not care.
He strolls through the jungle
waiting for what the future will bring.
The past he does not care.
The present, the past.

Victoria Clifford-Sanghad (11)
St John's RC Primary School, Bath

THE DARK FOREST IN MY HEAD

There's a dark, dark forest in my head,
Where trees whistle and wolves howl.
It sends a chill through my spine.
It's very, very dark in this forest of mine,
but in the day it's sunny and happy,
but then it gets dark and gloomy.

There's a dark, dark forest in my head,
where gloom hides the shadows.
It's very, very frightening in this forest of mine,
it frightens me almost to death.
'Creak, yikes, I'm out of here' I cried.
Running away.

Hannah Newman (9)
St John's RC Primary School, Bath

EARTH

Moon no longer seen,
No longer needed, a million street
Lamps glow peacefully.
A noise shatters the night, a bird is shot,
The last bird.
A long silence startles the earth.
Why can't people be gentle, why?
The streets are dull and grey.
Petrol fumes dance in the cool night air.
Each house has a light over every window.
What was once the countryside
Is now a block of flats.

Gabriella Brand (9)
St John's RC Primary School, Bath

THE EGYPTIAN CAT

The Egyptian cat
The Egyptian cat
Staring forever more
The Egyptian cat
The Egyptian cat
Soundless forever more
It can't move
It can't purr
Without movement forever more
The Egyptian cat
The Egyptian cat
Mummified in its tomb
The Egyptian cat
The Egyptian cat
Mummified forever more.

Zoe Wrigley (9)
St John's RC Primary School, Bath

BEGINNINGS

B   e quiet, someone is coming
E   verybody should be happy because they are alive
G   od has made you a very special person
I   'll come back very soon
N   ewborn people will know the truth
N   o badness will be in someone's heart
I   mmortality will come
N   obody will die
G   od loves you very much
S   in cannot be found in the world.

Jonathan Horsfall (10)
St John's RC Primary School, Bath

THE JUNGLE

Down in the jungle where nobody goes,
There lived a little monkey without any toes,
He went to the doctor and the doctor said,
'Hey Millie, we have to take of your leg.'

Down in the forest where nobody goes,
Lived a huge bear without a nose,
He went to the doctor and what did he say?
'Hey, your fur, it's gone all grey.'

Down beneath the ocean where nobody goes,
Lived a bubbly fish without any toes,
He went to the doctor and got out a plate,
He said 'You're a fish' and he ate him as steak.

Declan Stewart (10)
St John's RC Primary School, Bath

WINTER

Winter's cold of course you know,
You could make birds put on a show,
Birds like to eat seeds,
I am going to plant some weeds,
Snow comes down as quick as a flash,
I am going to make some mash,
When the rain comes down it goes into ice,
Yuck, look it's mice,
If you wish you can ski down the slopes,
But first it's up to the popes,
If you like you can go up the lift,
But mind it's quite a drift.

Kate Ealey (9)
St John's RC Primary School, Bath

NATURE

It is morning, the sun is just dawning,
And the blackbird is calling,
With the bugs crawling.

And the dolphins splashing against the waves,
And the gloomy caves,
Hiding from the waves.

And the different coloured sky,
Looking so bright,
With mighty light.

And the snakes that slither across the sand,
And the snakes are slithering
Deeper into the sand.

Behind the rocks there are
Some crocs,
Waiting for a meal.

Chloe Watson (9)
St John's RC Primary School, Bath

THE WATERFALL

Waterfalls spread over the rocks,
And spout over people's feet,
And blue and yellow colours,
Waterfalls splashing over people's feet,
And rising over rocks,
Twirling around and around in circles,
And slippery fish jumping up and down,
And spouting in people's face,
And rebounding against hard rocks.

Christopher Ballans (10)
St John's RC Primary School, Bath

Fog

Misty, opaque wind,
Cloaked in a grey fog,
Seeps in every corner.

An eerie silence
It stretches far and wide,
The houses look like they have sunk,
In a misty sea.

The colours blend into the fog,
The cold, dank blow of the powerful
Wind, floating above the land.

A gale of wind blows the trees,
Swiftly, side to side.

Joe Locke (9)
St John's RC Primary School, Bath

The Dark Wood

In the wood,
Where the trees howl,
And owls hoot like ghosts
One branch creaks,
I turn around,
Nothing there,
Must have been a mouse.
Bats are hanging upside down,
There's snakes around my feet,
I can hear the
Crickets whistling.

John-Paul Indoe (10)
St John's RC Primary School, Bath

PERPETUAL TWILIGHT

Once I remember
What it was like,
Beautiful colours,
Shimmered throughout the world,
Now I'm just alone.

With no one to play with,
Just stone and rubble,
Will I ever see life,
Not me, not ever,
I wish I could lay
On green grass forever,
And just dream.

I might as well go,
With no one to know,
Life's pretty boring.

Tom DeMichele (10)
St John's RC Primary School, Bath

WEATHER

I walk through the autumn leaves crunching,
Round and through my feet, and trees swaying
Like water from side to side as the autumn leaves
Speed to the ground, the colours shimmer throughout
The world.

The white snow falling with my feet
Sloshing, splashing through the snow,
With children playing snowfights.

Kieren Davies (10)
St John's RC Primary School, Bath

IMAGINE

I stepped out of my house into the night,
The cold air blew my face, I shivered.
The leaves rustled, I got goosebumps,
A gun went bang, a black shadow fell.
Sorrow was in my heart.
I was scared, I imagined what would happen
If all the animals were killed.
Everyone would cry, everyone would feel the loss.
Why did people make guns, to kill animals of course.
Just imagine if you were an elephant.,
People want your ivory. They shoot you with a gun. *Bang!*
You are dead, how would you like it?
Well, I would not. So please don't kill the animals.
Please?

Louisa Prentice (10)
St John's RC Primary School, Bath

I REMEMBER

I remember what it was like
To walk on a sandy beach.
I remember when I could swim,
In a deep, dark, blue ocean.
I remember when it was transparent air,
I remember when there were sea animals alive.
I remember when it was the countryside,
And not skyscrapers, car fumes,
Big, black and rotten buildings.
I remember when it was a sunset,
And not a gloomy day.
The environment has been destroyed!

Sinead Rowland (10)
St John's RC Primary School, Bath

WORLD WAR

The year 1943
I hear nothing but guns,
Why me?
Why not someone else?
It's not fair.
I did nothing to deserve this,
It just isn't right,
It shouldn't be happening,
Why war?
My home has gone,
My family have died,
Why me?
People cry to see their death,
Nothing can be done.

Jolene Hartrey (10)
St John's RC Primary School, Bath

SILENT AND STILL

Silent and still,
The secret world of our past,
The dusty treasures of mankind,
Seeking out what's left,
What's left of what?
We don't know.

Silent and still,
Pushing through the misty depths of time,
But now we must go,
Leave our past,
Creep into the future,
Silent and still.

Rebecca Morgan (10)
St John's RC Primary School, Bath

A VIEW FROM A RAT

I sneak,
I creep,
Among the rubbish bins,
Apple cores, liquid from a can, and the odd banana skin,
Mouldy cornflakes and half-eaten chocolate bars,
Leftover jam in cracked glass jars.

I sneak,
I creep,
Along the dirty street,
Stuck down bubblegum, sticky paper bags with the odd sweet inside,
Getting fruit from the humans, that's what I tried.

I sneak,
I creep,
Along the filthy park,
Sneaking, creeping when it's nearly dark,
Dropped lollipops,
And a bag of chocolate drops.

Rosaline Dolton (9)
St John's RC Primary School, Bath

A WONDERFUL WORLD

No more guns, no war,
No more killing the world,
Less wounding the world.

Destroying ourselves,
Pollution in the water,
Crumbling the earth.

Liam McSherry (9)
St John's RC Primary School, Bath

WORLD WAR TWO

I write to my family every day,
Thinking as I write,
Any minute the war will end,
Any day now.
I don't get any sleep during the night,
'Cause of all the bombing.
My children are very young,
They wouldn't understand.
I hope every minute of the day
That we can get through this.
Bombs are exploding every second of the day.
Silence for a few seconds,
Then screams of pain
Are heard throughout the battlefield.

Charles Perry (11)
St John's RC Primary School, Bath

GHOST

In the night when everyone is asleep,
The moon comes out, owls hooting, hooting.
Swiftly, swiftly, the fox's searching,
Searching around for food.
The cars stop in the drive at night,
And the owls stop,
Ghost quickly in and out of the house.

They're like fog,
Fog indeed
When the sun comes out,
The ghosts go back to their graves.

Kyle Stone (10)
St John's RC Primary School, Bath

FUTURE

Here I am, back after two hundred years,
Everything looks the same,
But there's a lot of cobwebs.

I remember the good old days,
Sat at my desk thinking
'What is she going on about?'

Look, the date's still on the board,
Mrs Randall must have forgotten
To rub it off.

Mrs Randall has still got
The fractions on the wall,
And all our work.
Yes, I remember. I remember
Zzzzzzzz

Charlotte Moon (10)
St John's RC Primary School, Bath

SILENCE

The war is over,
The guns have stopped,
It all fell to silence,
As I walked along the trench.

People all around me,
Silent as can be,
Soldiers dead and families sad,
As sad as can be.

Silence is scary,
Silence is war,
But after I realised,
There wasn't any more.

Soldiers started praying,
Then we heard a cheer,
The war is over maties,
There's silence over here.

Chloe Ridley (10)
St John's RC Primary School, Bath

A SONG FOR SPRING

Spring, a time of merry laughing,
Spring, a time of joyous dancing,
Spring with flowers, pink and blue,
Spring, a time for me and you.

Spring, a time for bunny rabbits,
Spring a time for new habits,
Spring, a time for daffodils,
Spring a place of new thrills.

Spring, a time to have fun,
Spring, a time for everyone,
Spring, a time to run and hop,
Spring, a time to bop, bop, bop.

Spring, a time to use your voice,
Spring, a time to rejoice,
Spring, a time for happiness,
Spring, a time to clean up your mess.

Adam Kingston (10)
St John's RC Primary School, Bath

BACK WHEN THE WORLD WAS SILENCED

The sirens ear-piercing,
War is upon us,
No, not again.
This is the last time,
I hope,
It has to be,
One last time I hear it,
The screeching.
Like a song bird,
But none live here,
I've been through it,
I lived through it,
I will survive.

Samuel Crook (11)
St John's RC Primary School, Bath

WAR MEMORIES

I look out of the window
I can still hear gun shots in my head,
Even though the guns have gone.
Everyone is celebrating because the war has ended,
And their husbands have come back.
I'm not, I'm waiting for my son,
Even though he is dead.
I walk through the graveyard,
Beautiful flowers on every grave,
But one hasn't. I walk up to it,
It is my son's.
Why can't I join my friends in heaven?

Alexander Johnson (11)
St John's RC Primary School, Bath

MY PAST, PRESENT AND FUTURE

My past has gone,
My future is coming,
My present will never end.

The millennium is coming,
But what will happen between this time and that.
I don't know what will happen in my future,
I may regret it,
I may enjoy it.

Exciting, disappointing, wonderful,
I look back at my life,
And feel these feelings.

Past, present and future,
Only one of these you will ever know.

Hannah Piekarski (10)
St John's RC Primary School, Bath

OUR WORLD

Cutting down our trees,
We are unable to breathe,
They produce our air.

Preserving our world,
Killing plants and animals,
I don't think it's right.

Polluted rivers,
Being cruel to our world,
It might cause a fight.

Olivia Cundy (8)
St John's RC Primary School, Bath

SPRING

The flowers are growin'
But it's a bad time if it's snowin'
In the summer time,
There are loads of trees to climb.

You can sunbathe outside,
And you can have chips that are fried,
There's nothing to it, you just have
To do work about gardens a bit.

When you've finished it,
And now you're a full gardener,
You've got some nice kit.
And now it looks lovely,
It's nice and snuggly!

William Butler (10)
St John's RC Primary School, Bath

WHY

Is the future a thing you are scared of!
Will we have webbed feet or
Will we be floating in the air!
No one knows.
Why!
Why are we going to the moon and finding new things!
Why!
Why is there time!
Why do we not know the answers to the questions
We keep asking ourselves.
Why is there life.
Why!

Danielle Bolton (10)
St John's RC Primary School, Bath

A PERFECT WORLD

Wars can be stopped,
Stop cutting down trees,
Care for our street and no disease,
Will the sea be clean.

Joe Shannon (8)
St John's RC Primary School, Bath

CLEAN

Clean water can be nice,
Dirty water makes you ill,
Clean is way better.

Liam Perdicchia (9)
St John's RC Primary School, Bath

AN ANIMAL'S WORLD

If our world was kind,
Animals would be alive,
And not killed at all.

Hazel Walker (9)
St John's RC Primary School, Bath

THE SUN WOULD SHOW IF . . .

Stop polluting air,
If only that could happen,
The sun would show light.

James Ellis (9)
St John's RC Primary School, Bath

THE BAT

I, the bat,
In the dark, damp night,
What a fright,
Flying through the night.

I, the bat, eat the fruit of the trees,
And I fly through the breeze,
I, the bat, through the night,
My dark skin keeps me out of sight,
I sleep in the morning,
I creep in the night,
I, the bat,
What a fright,
Flying through the dark, damp night.

Liam Hopkinson (11)
St John's RC Primary School, Bath

A PERFECT WORLD

I like the raindrops
I like it when the rain goes
I do like the plants.

I do like the sun
I do like the rain and plants
I like the blueberries.

The sun shines on me
I like the sun and the rain
I like the sunshine.

Alana King (8)
St John's RC Primary School, Bath

CHILDHOOD

Childhood is like . . .
A strike of lightning,
A wave of excitement,
A beam of sunshine.

Childhood is like . . .
A rain fall's glitter,
The dust rubbed off fairies' wings,
A puddle of tears.

Childhood is like . . .
A bent building,
An everlasting gobstopper,
A pen that sprays gold.

Childhood is . . .
Made of many ingredients,
A down stream flowing rainbow,
A dream come true.

Childhood is like . . .
A vertical line with bumps in.

Lisa Advani (11)
St John's RC Primary School, Bath

SUN AND RAIN

When the rain splashes,
And the sun shines so bright,
When the rainbow comes.

I see the snow fall,
Snowballs being thrown past me,
I see the snow go.

Theodore Alexander (8)
St John's RC Primary School, Bath

THE MILLENNIUM CELEBRATION

The night waits for the new day,
A special day,
Shivering with freezing icicles,
Digging into the wind,
Everyone waits patiently,
Watching the clock,
Eyes stare,
Cheers wait,
Hands on the bubbling champagne,
You wait to see if the lights are going to go out,
Burning candles flicker in the misty silence,
You freeze to see when the clock will strike twelve,
The first chime goes off *ding*,
The second chime goes off *dong*,
The third chime goes off *ding*,
You gasp at the fourth *dong*,
Then you wait two seconds,
Someone shouts,
The lights are still here,
Hooray everyone cheers,
Children dance,
Cheer and laugh,
Yes, yes, the millennium's here,
Adults pop champagne and the bubbles fly,
Balloons glide swiftly through the midnight sky,
The girls do cartwheels,
The people of the city are relieved.

Virginia Golf (9)
St John's RC Primary School, Bath

WITH SUNLIGHT

As I sit here in the classroom,
With sunlight gently filtering through,
I can imagine that I'm on a remote island,
Lying on a silvery beach,
While soft diamonds of sand swirl amazingly around me,
And the sea lapping peacefully beside.

As I sit here in the classroom,
With the sunlight warmly seeping through,
I can imagine an evil monster,
Namely, pollution,
That we all must pull together to fight,
Or the foundations of a green world for the future,
Will crumble and fall.

As I sit here in the classroom,
With sunlight brightly droning on,
I can imagine a giant book of sums,
I flee in terror!
1,226 divided by 5?
More maths than ever,
A teetering pile falling down and crushing me!

As I sit here in the classroom,
With the sunlight dreamily smiling through,
I can imagine a huge book,
This book is the best I've ever read,
Everything a good book is made of,
One that you can't put down.

As I sit here in the classroom,
With sunlight happily gazing at me,
I can imagine anything,
Because the sunlight made it possible.

Emma Proctor (11)
St John's RC Primary School, Bath

THE GHOST IN THE CASTLE

I'm the ghost in the castle,
Colonel Fazackerly is there,
I'm going to scare him,
This time, yes I will,
Colonel Fazackerly beware.

I'm the ghost in the castle,
Boo Colonel, *Boo* Colonel, *Boo.*
Oh little ghost, you do not scare me,
Well . . . well . . . well . . . Colonel Fazackerly beware.

I'm the ghost in the castle,
I'll rattle my bones till he drops,
Oh little ghost you just will not scare me,
you are so amusing,
To a fellow like me.

I'm the ghost in the castle,
I will leave this castle right now,
He has made me unhappy,
I just cannot bear it,
Colonel Fazackerly . . . please *beware!*

Milly Gladwin (11)
St John's RC Primary School, Bath

SPRING

Rain as soft as silk
Spring is coming to an end
So we will rejoice.

Marc Morgan (8)
St John's RC Primary School, Bath

THE SEASONS

Spring . . .
In the spring,
The daffodils grow,
And everything does,
But very slow.

Summer . . .
Then summer comes,
And you play outside,
You go to the beach,
And you swim in the tide.

Autumn . . .
Then autumn comes,
And the leaves go brown,
You play in them,
Like a silly clown.

Winter . . .
In the winter,
The flowers stop growing,
And all the time,
It's always snowing.

Christopher Brain (11)
St John's RC Primary School, Bath

A PERFECT WORLD

No more polluting,
No more shooting animals,
Save the rainforests.

Julian Richardson (9)
St John's RC Primary School, Bath

My Dad

My dad is really embarrassing,
He tells everyone my secrets,
Especially at parent's evening,
He writes on the board, 'Hi Natalie, dad,'
It's so embarrassing,
Everyone's talking about it.

When my friends come round,
He always tells jokes about me,
And if I have something new,
He always makes fun of me,
I'll get my revenge one day.

On my birthday he let me have
Two friends to stay over.
He gave them two herb sausages each,
And in the middle of the night,
My friends both threw up all over me.
How embarrassing!
That's what my dad's like.

Natalie Reid (10)
St John's RC Primary School, Bath

Home

My favourite place is home,
It's cosy and comfy,
Warm and lovely.

My favourite things are there,
There's books and toys.
It's my favourite place.

Claire Summerfield (10)
St John's RC Primary School, Bath

ALL THE PLANETS IN THE WORLD

Mars, Venus and Jupiter,
Mars is for war,
Venus is for love,
And Jupiter is for happiness.

All these planets,
Are above us in the sky.
We are down here on the ground,
In our own little world.

But is there another world,
Somewhere up high in the sky.
Maybe there is, maybe there isn't,
But what would it be like,
In other people's worlds.

Would it be weird,
Or would it be cool,
Will we ever know?

Charlotte Perry (11)
St John's RC Primary School, Bath

DAFFODILS

D   elightful when the sun is out,
A   lways very pretty,
F   abulous all the time,
F   resh and lovely,
O   range in the middle,
D   affodils are wonderful,
I   love them all the time,
L   ovely in the spring!

Henrietta Forsyth (11)
St John's RC Primary School, Bath

I AM THE BEST

I won the Olympic Games,
I won a tennis match,
I won the swimming race,
And the running race.

I won the yo-yo competition,
And the cycling race,
I won a football match,
I won a hockey match.

I was the best,
But when I woke up,
I found it all a dream.

Thomas Menezes (10)
St John's RC Primary School, Bath

THE SEASIDE

The sea crashing and bashing around my feet.
This is my favourite place to meet,
Building castles in the sand,
The sun shining all day long,
Laughing, playing, swimming in the sea,
Eating picnics and ice-creams,
This fills me with glee,
Collecting pebbles and shells,
To take them home,
This is the best day for me.

Lucy Baker (9)
St John's RC Primary School, Bath

WAR

War, it is a dreadful thing, people dying everywhere,
As a damp, dark, misty day,
People are crying and people are dead.
Burned-down shops and burned down trees,
And this used to be a wonderful place.
People in hunger all night and day.
War, war is a horrible thing.
A ditch with dead people is a horrible thing.
War, war, I don't believe it even started.
War, war, it is cold blooded.
War means evil things to people
Who it comes to.
War, war, will it ever end.

Nicholas Harding (10)
St John's RC Primary School, Bath

THE RAIN

The rain comes from the sky,
It comes from right up high.

The rain comes,
Rolls down the lane,
And it will drip,
Down the drain.

The rain comes,
Makes lots of puddles,
The children splash about,
And play nearly all day.

Daniel Fubara (11)
St John's RC Primary School, Bath

SPRING

The sun has come,
It's time for fun,
Flowers sprouting,
Children shouting,
People lying in the park.

Bees buzzing,
Grown-ups humming,
People running everywhere,
Spring has come,
Fun, fun, fun.

Babies playing,
People praying,
Easter eggs,
All is here,
The spring air,
Hum, hum,
I would give anything for spring to come again.

Talitha Alexander (10)
St John's RC Primary School, Bath

THE MILLENNIUM BUG

Mr Buggy what will you do?
I will eat your computers and make you blue,
Eat your electrics and ruin the fun,
And I will blow your house up with my gun,
Oh Mr Buggy, do not do that,
Or I'll stomp on you,
And that will be that.

Zoe Wood (7)
St Joseph's & St Teresa's RC VA School, Wells

GADGETS

Heads and hands put together,
What shall I do this millennium?
Should I buy a robot and a flying car?
Or the millennium star?
It's so hard,
Heads and hands put together,
What shall I do this millennium?
Shall I save computers from the
Millennium Bug?
And make everyone hug?
I'm going insane!
Oh please don't rain.
You'll scramble up my brain,
Heads and hands put together,
What shall I do this millennium?

Kimberley Beer (9)
St Joseph's & St Teresa's RC VA School, Wells

BONKER BUGGY

Oh Millennium Bug what will you bring?
Will you be good or will you be bad?
I will be bad and spoil your fun,
You won't have electricity any more.
How will you be bad?
What will you break?
I will break your computers, lights and TV.
How can you spoil our celebration and our jubilation?
I will spoil your celebration and jubilation by
Disconnecting your computers, CD players and lights.

Mathew Jessop (8)
St Joseph's & St Teresa's RC VA School, Wells

CELEBRATION

Food and drink, drink and food,
Everyone is eating food.
It's twelve o'clock,
And everybody knows it's not time to stop.
Party poppers go pop!
When it's twelve o'clock,
And everybody stops.
Oh good, oh good, it's millennium time,
It's gone past twelve,
Party poppers go pop!
When it's twelve o'clock.
Corks go pop! Party poppers go pop!
Oh good, it's party time.
Party poppers go pop!
When it's twelve o'clock.

Natalie Hicks (9)
St Joseph's & St Teresa's RC VA School, Wells

THE MILLENNIUM

One day I went down to the rubbish dump,
And to my surprise saw a heffalump.
He was dancing, dancing, I don't know why
And he said the millennium was nearby.
He said it is a special time,
And it will start when the bells go chime.
Then suddenly the bells did chime.
He said hooray, hooray, it's millennium time.

Edmund Bevan (8)
St Joseph's & St Teresa's RC VA School, Wells

MILLENNIUM CELEBRATIONS

Screaming and shouting, everything's fun,
So come to the party and have good fun.

Party poppers are going,
Blowers are blowing,
Come and join the fun,
For it's time to get going.

The candles are lit, the cake comes through,
Everyone's singing and dancing too.

Party poppers are going,
Blowers are blowing,
Come and join the fun,
For it's time to get going.

We play lots of games and
Call each other names.

Party poppers are going,
Blowers are blowing,
Come and join the fun,
For it's time to get going.

Patricia Williams (9)
St Joseph's & St Teresa's RC VA School, Wells

MILLENNIUM BUG

Oh dear, oh dear, the millennium's here.
We're saying that, for the bug is near.
Please stop, you'll spoil our fun
Lots of buns for everyone.
The bells will chime.
When it's millennium time.

Amy Burfield (9)
St Joseph's & St Teresa's RC VA School, Wells

MILLENNIUM BUG

Millennium Bug please don't spoil my fun.
Because I think computers are number one.
No! No! No! You silly person don't cry,
It won't help so,
Stop your crying,
Stop it at once,
Or there'll be
No celebration,
There won't be a single electric light,
And it'll seem like night,
I told you, you silly person, don't cry,
It won't help so
Stop your crying,
Stop it at once,
Or there'll be
No celebration,
Oh, there goes the clock chime, yes, it's destroying time,
Oh no you don't, and I squashed him flat so,
Stop your crying,
Stop it at once,
Or there'll be
No celebration.

Maxwell Jeffery (8)
St Joseph's & St Teresa's RC VA School, Wells

CELEBRATIONS FOR THE MILLENNIUM

Hoorah, hoorah, it's party time.
The millennium is here hoorah!
Hoorah, hoorah, it's party time.
Let's celebrate, hoorah!

Hoorah, hoorah, it's party time.
Let's open our presents, hoorah!
Hoorah, hoorah it's party time.
Let's pull our crackers, hoorah!

Alexander Mitchell (9)
St Joseph's & St Teresa's RC VA School, Wells

OH BUGGY

Oh Buggy, oh Buggy what will you do?
Will you turn me into an elephant
and send me to the zoo.
Oh no, oh no, I won't do that.
I'll just sit back and that is that.
Oh Buggy, oh Buggy, where will you be
When the millennium comes to me.
I'll just sit down and cuddle my clown.
Oh Buggy, oh Buggy, I've decided to see you as my pet.
So I'm going to catch you on my Internet.

Elspeth Maguire (8)
St Joseph's & St Teresa's RC VA School, Wells

MILLENNIUM CELEBRATIONS

Food and drink are part of the party.
The main attraction is karate.
People climbing trees and hedges.
People going off their edges.
Tony Blair is dancing in a boogie manner.
Everyone's seen the millennium banner.
Now we'll have some cod in batter.
The Millennium Bug will not matter.

Alberic Elsom (9)
St Joseph's & St Teresa's RC VA School, Wells

MILLENNIUM

Gadgets and disasters, everything's the master's.
The Bug is smashing everything.
He can't stop it, but he likes to bite.
Please help us to remove him.
I went to the man in the flat below,
I asked him why he had a bow.
Why kid, don't you know, *ho, ho, ho.*
It's the millennium.
What have I done,
Oh no, I haven't made cakes for anyone.
Don't worry kid, there is nothing to do.
OK then, I'll sit with you.

Ian Butcher (9)
St Joseph's & St Teresa's RC VA School, Wells

MILLENNIUM TIME

Hooray, hoorah, the millennium's come.
Lots of parties and lots of fun.
Crowds of people celebrating,
many, many generations.
And when it is millennium time,
the midnight bells will start to chime.
Everyone will drink some wine.
Hoorah, hooray, it's millennium time.

William Chivers (8)
St Joseph's & St Teresa's RC VA School, Wells

PARTY TIME

Good, oh good, it's millennium time,
Come on, I want to hear the twelfth chime,
Come on it's time to play and run,
I want to have a feast with a big, fat bun,
Everybody was chewing food,
Everybody was listening to music and going 'cool dude.'
Come, it's time to play and run,
I want to have a feast with a big, fat bun.
It's millennium time, everybody's being insane,
I don't know if my brain can contain that much,
Come on it's time to play and run,
I want to have a feast with a big, fat bun.

Courtenay Gadd (8)
St Joseph's & St Teresa's RC VA School, Wells

MILLENNIUM VEHICLES

Solar vehicles rushing by.
Let's go and have the futuristic ride.
The new solar vehicles are here because
Of the Millennium Bug, Bug, Bug.
Solar trains speeding by.
Old trains in the scrapyard, yes.
Then overhead roars a plane.
The new solar-powered kind.
Concorde's in a museum.
A new Concorde's been built.

Thomas Dalton (8)
St Joseph's & St Teresa's RC VA School, Wells

MILLENNIUM

Good, o good, the time has come,
Now it's time for lots of fun,
Now its time to run and play,
I heard lots of horses and they all went *neigh*.
Foot to foot and hand to hand,
Everyone is dancing to a band.
It's time for the poppers, wine and juice,
Some are excited, are eating goose.
Millennium is here, it's such good fun,
Girls were shouting, come, come, come,
Hurray, hurray the people cry,
They all were so happy, they think they can fly.

Martha O'Connell (7)
St Joseph's & St Teresa's RC VA School, Wells

YEAR 2000

Robbie Williams making songs,
Millennium Dome on its way.
Another century has passed,
Won't that make my day?
The future's getting closer,
New things being made,
Good things to look forward to,
So the olden days will fade.

Callum Mays (8)
St Joseph's & St Teresa's RC VA School, Wells

PARTY TIME

Buggy bug, don't ruin the millennium,
Make it a celebration,
And help me to do the decoration,
And with the party clothes,
Don't forget it is year 2000,
Oh, oh, buggy bug, do you want
To be in touch on the Internet?

Jamie O'Neill (7)
St Joseph's & St Teresa's RC VA School, Wells

ANOTHER YEAR

It's another year,
but this time
the millennium is here!
Laughing, dancing, having lots of fun,
staying up late for everyone.

We can make this millennium a special year.
We can help the poor people terrified with fear.
The Third World has a huge debt,
that we should all forget.
So that they can start anew,
to make the future for them good too.
If we worked together as a team,
the world can be -
clean and green.

If you are interested in helping the world be a better place,
go on you could be a hero,
then call me on my mobile -
two, zero, zero, zero!
(2000)

Becky Collins (10)
Wells Cathedral School

THE MILLENNIUM BUG

Millennium, Millennium Bug,
This isn't a cute one that's snug in a rug.
This one's set off by the changing date,
If you've got an old machine you're a bit too late.
It'll make all the old computers crash,
All of them will turn into trash.

Millennium, millennium, the Millennium Bug,
This isn't a cute one that's snug in a rug.
It'll make all the computers go crazy,
'Cos the old designers were being lazy.
They made it only a two digit date,
Now we know that wasn't too great.

Millennium, millennium, the Millennium Bug,
This isn't a cute one that's snug in a rug.
It isn't just computers that will be affected,
Loads of appliances could be infected.
VCRs and burglar alarms could go as well,
Your life might be as bad as hell.

Matthew Baker (10)
Widcombe CE Junior School

FIGHT FOR YOUR COUNTRY

Colds, deaths, broken bones,
Blood, flesh, crying for home.
Flying high up in the air,
Necks are sweaty with stood up hair.

Mourning over relative's deaths,
Is no use when they don't have any breath.
Crying, crying, shed those tears.
Crying, crying, for your dears.

Nervous and exciting sighs,
Keeps you bravely flying high.
Don't give up and never turn back,
Shoot those Nazis, don't give the slack.

Give it a go and give it a try,
Never be gloomy and think that you'll die.
Fight for your country and fight for your lives,
Keep looking forward and you will survive.

Yang Bo (10)
Widcombe CE Junior School

THE SEA CREATURES

All the creatures in the sea,
At 9.00 o'clock they have their tea.
The dolphin is the mother cook,
Her husband is a very bad crook.
He goes every day to the shore,
To see what meat is in store.
Because he is a Great White shark,
His best food is a singing lark.

All the creatures in the sea,
At 9:00 o'clock they have their tea.
The jellyfish they like the most,
Because he makes them laugh when dancing on a post.
He is the sea's minstrel.
That's why they all call him Tinstrel.
He has a clever wife,
She is very good for advice.

Nina Smith Stevens (10)
Widcombe CE Junior School

FIREWORKS

Swirls, bangs, fireworks and more.
Bonfires, sweeties and Guy Fawkes galore!

Everybody's cheering - *ooh and aah!*
Here's a roman candle, light now dark.

To finish off the night, the big one's
coming up . . .
Here it goes - *whoosh*
                bang
                  fizz
                    flash
                      crackle
                        swirl . . .
All until next year!

Toby Gale (10)
Widcombe CE Junior School

MY AFTER CHRISTMAS POEM

Christmas had come,
people had fun.
Angels on trees,
as Christmas flees.
People partied,
children smartied.
Clocks chimed,
had a good time.
The Christmas dove,
sent lots of love.
Christmas had gone,
sang a song.

Arfa Cameron (11)
Widcombe CE Junior School

YETI

The yeti is called Bigfoot,
'Though his feet aren't very big.
He normally feasts on mountain goats,
But he also likes wild pig.

The yeti lives in mountains,
Probably all alone.
He might have one or two yeti friends,
But if he does they're all unknown.

The yeti has a giant throat,
He never, ever chokes,
He could be very friendly,
He could be a big hoax.

Greg Feldwick (10)
Widcombe CE Junior School

PARENTS' EVENING

'It's parents' evening on Thursday,' the teacher said.
I covered my face with my book, I went bright red.
I tried to go home without a letter,
But she said I'd better.
I screwed it up in my pocket and forgot to take it out.
My mum found it, oh boy! Oh boy! Did she shout.
I was grounded for the week
not even allowed to speak.
But when the day came
everything was the same.
She's forgotten all about it,
why did I ever doubt it.

Scarlett Christley (9)
Widcombe CE Junior School

THE THREE-EYED BUDGIE

There's a three-eyed budgie in my school,
The teachers call him a fool.

The budgie is all very clever,
Because he lives on pieces of leather.

He can talk,
And he can walk.

That's why they called him clever,
But the teacher says I'm better.

The budgie flew out of its cage,
The teacher stormed out in a rage.

'I hate that budgie,' the teacher said.
'I'm going off to bed!'

The children cheered, 'Hooray, hooray!'
Soon it was the end of the day.

The boy switched out the lights,
And said to the budgie, 'Night, night!'

Rachel Bird (10)
Widcombe CE Junior School

THE REAL, REAL SEA

Where the waves break
Where the winds roar
Where the beach grows cold
Is the real, real sea.

Where the jellyfish lie
Where you see a crab's claw
Where you have sand on your feet
Is the real, real sea.

Where the pebbles are small
And the shells are beautiful
Where the sand grows soft
Is the real, real sea.

Where the dunes are green
You will find the queen
Of the sand, the shells and the sea.
That's when you'll know you're at
The real, real sea.

Rachel Morgan (8)
Widcombe CE Junior School

OLD-TIMER

Here comes the old-timer,
Chug, chug, chug, bang. Chug, chug, chug, bang.
Spurting and spluttering, *'Splutter, splutter,*
Chug, chug, chug, bang. Chug, chug, chug, bang.'

He is the oldest car around,
Chug, chug, chug, bang. Chug, chug, chug, bang.
Listen to that horrible sound,
Chug, chug, chug, bang. Chug, chug, chug, bang.

All the other cars spread around,
Peep, peep.
When they hear that horrible sound,
Beep, beep.

They can't bear that horrible smell,
Chug, chug, chug, bang. Chug, chug, chug, bang.
Now that's the car nobody would dare to sell,
Chug, chug, chug, bang. Chug, chug, chug bang.

Emily Harrison (8)
Widcombe CE Junior School

SLOW SNAILS

Walking down the garden path
were some slippery, slow snails.
Slip, slip, sliperroo
Go the snails on the garden path.

Over the moss
Across the slab
And in the gardener's house.

The snails are slow . . .
Not quick!
Slip, slip, sliperroo
Go the snails on the garden path.

Over the moss
Across the slab
And in the gardener's house.

The snails are so slow
So tired and so slow
slip . . . slip . . . sliperroo . . .

Alice Corp (8)
Widcombe CE Junior School

MIKE

There was once a boy called Mike.
Who was excellent on his bike.
He did a big jump
Landing on his head with a thump.
Then he decided to play with his kite.

Michael Carter (9)
Widcombe CE Junior School

WINTER DAYS

When it comes to wintertime
  it starts a strong wind blowing
But it gets wet, you won't regret
  because then it starts snowing.

Because all week it gets so cold
  I would say it's freezing.
Because my mother is so ill
  she's sneezing, sneezing, sneezing!

And how come it's so cold outside?
  We have to sit round the fire -
There's nothing else to do all day
  but watch the flames grow higher.

And when the snow is thick enough,
  the animals hibernate.
What do they do all winter day?
  They close their eyes and wait.

But when I look outside each day
  I see the robin singing.
That's when the day's beginning
  and I hear the church bells ringing.

Phoebe Jelley (9)
Widcombe CE Junior School

MY POEM

The moon came down
And the sun came up
then all the flowers appeared
and all the children turned up with toys.

Cosmo Born (8)
Widcombe CE Junior School

MEGAN MY NEW COUSIN

It took ages for the new baby to come
When will it be born
Kicking, pushing and pressing
Will it be a girl or boy

When will it be born
Ting-a-ling the telephone rings
I picked up the phone and heard
It's a girl and Megan's her name

Tiny hands and tiny toes
She has rosy cheeks and a little nose
She loves her milk and her cosy bed
I love my baby Megan

Alice Phillips (8)
Widcombe CE Junior School

MR WINKY

Mr Winky hangs on the wall
Holding his big red ball.
But when all the children have gone back home
He'll ring his mum on the telephone.
Occasionally Mr Winky will wink
But he gets so embarrassed and his nose turns pink.
Blame it on the children for pulling him
And I'll tell you now he's not very slim.
Oh poor Mr Winky who hangs on the wall
That's probably why he is so small.

Kate Cantell (10)
Widcombe CE Junior School

BANANAS

Bananas are deliciously yummy,
They are soft and yellow and slide down to my tummy.
They're not my favourite I have to say,
But I still might eat them every day.

Monkeys like bananas, they like them best.
My brother likes them and he's a pest.
Monkeys and pests belong in the zoo,
Maybe my brother belongs there too.

But I like my brother better than bananas,
Especially when he's in his pyjamas.
We're ready for bed, we've had our tea,
We've both had bananas him and me.

Jennifer Humphreys   (8)
Widcombe CE Junior School

ALL BECAUSE OF THE PEAR

I eat a big pear.
The pear had a hair.
I had a tickle
It was like pickle.
I wish I did not eat that pear
With that hair
I hate the tickle
But I like the sound of the pickle
I'm hungry
I'll have a pear.

Angus Rodger (9)
Widcombe CE Junior School

UNTITLED . . .

1, 2, 3, 4
Let me have the zooming door.
5, 6, 7, 8
You know that I want a plate.
9, 10, 11, 12
My brother is a little elf.
13, 14, 15, 16
Stop being so very mean.
17, 18, 19, 20
Hey! Hey! Isn't that plenty.
21, 22, 23, 24
I have got a large bag of straw.
25, 26, 27, 28
I go to Roller Mania to have a good skate.

Courtney Campbell
Widcombe CE Junior School

A FROG

His is big!
He has a wig!

He is fat!
He has a big hat!

He is great!
He has one good mate!

He likes the sun!
He can be fat like a bun.

Alexander Dale-Staples (8)
Widcombe CE Junior School

THE MYSTIC LAND

There once was a land
Everywhere was sand
But magic dust appeared
Everywhere.

There was an animal called Midget
(Who was also known as Widget).
Who sang a sweet serenade.
A lovely song.

'Oh lovely mystic land,
Please come and hold my hand
And let's go away,
And go around the world.

Luna Rusk (8)
Widcombe CE Junior School

MY DOG

My dog, my dog,
ate a frog.

My dog, my dog was sick,
so my rabbit gave it a kick.

My dog, my dog, needed the bog.
My dog, my dog brought in a log.

My dog, my dog sat on a wall.
My dog, my dog went to a ball.

My dog, my dog ate my teddy.
My dog, my dog is always ready.

Jessica Smith (10)
Widcombe CE Junior School

THE ALIEN SPACESHIP

Once I saw a UFO
It was flying very low.

I saw an alien inside the ship,
Small and as dainty as a microchip.

I said to myself, it might come from Mars,
For its spaceship was as big as three hundred cars.

The ship was the most fantastic colours,
In fact it looked like there were no others.

In some places it's circled, in others it's square,
In the side of the ship there's a very big tear.

I watched for a while in the fading light,
But then the ship flew out of sight.

Gabrielle Fisher (10)
Widcombe CE Junior School

THE SUN

The sun is very bright.
It gives us lots of light.
It goes down at night.

The moon comes up instead.
When you are all in bed.

In the morning the sun comes up.
It somehow looks like a great big teacup.

Maisie Bygraves (8)
Widcombe CE Junior School

THE UNIVERSE

Yesterday I went to the stars,
Then I took a trip to Mars,
I discovered a planet called Zom,
In the air was a nuclear bomb.
Next I went to the black hole,
And then I saw a flying mole.

Also I went to Planet Venus,
I saw an alien who was called Janus.
Then I went into the alien's hut,
Next I drank a drink called Mut.
I said goodbye to the alien.
Then I saw the alien wailing.

Next I went to the planet Pluto,
When I was there I drank some Duco.
Then I went to Planet Neptune,
I ate my only prune.
After that I went to Planet Saturn,
Which had a lot of coloured patterns.

Then I went to Planet Mercury,
Next I ate a big fat turkey.
I then went to Planet Jupiter,
There I bought a bicycle hooter.
Then I went to Planet Uranus,
In the distance I could see Planet Venus.

Afterward I went to Planet Earth,
My wife there had a sudden birth.
Then I saw a little rabbit,
It was eating in a disgusting habit
And in my country called Rome,
I made myself feel more at home.

Rosemary Hawkins (9)
Widcombe CE Junior School

MY FIRST RACE

I'll never forget my first ever race,
it was cool . . . it was ace!
I had to wear a special suit,
crash helmet to protect my head,
in case I crashed and ended up dead.

I was really nervous and very scared,
butterflies forming in my tummy and head.
The lights went red and then to green,
off I went in my go-kart machine.

Unfortunately I did not win,
but I got a medal which made me grin.
Then I went home and went to bed,
with thoughts of speed in my head.

Enzo Cavaliero (10)
Widcombe CE Junior School

ROCKET

Rocket, rocket flying by,
How you do zoom and fly.
Like a star in the sky.
In space we've landed on the moon,
Like a huge grizzly baboon.
You would be burnt by the sun,
Then baked like a bun.
When you've been up,
You'd go down,
rocket,
rocket,
rocket,
rocket.

Gareth Hobbs (7)
Widcombe CE Junior School

MY CAT

My cat is black,
he is so fat.
Every day he pats
the other cats.
He plays with string.
When he sees a rat.
He chases it round the ring.

Ryan Blackman (7)
Widcombe CE Junior School

CHEETAH THE FAST

Has a spotty body
He has two lines going from his eyes
stopping by his nose.
He has pale green eyes.
He has a slinky body.

Daniel Jennings (7)
Widcombe CE Junior School

PROGRESS

2000 millennium
1000 years ago
when people used carts to get to and fro.
Now we have cars to get from side to side.
They are nationwide.

Elly Jones (9)
Widcombe CE Junior School

OUT IN SPACE

Out in space
there are lots of stars
but up there
absolutely no cars.
(Unless one floated up).

Claire Jones (8)
Widcombe CE Junior School

FOOTBALL

Football is brilliant
Football is cool
Football is skill
Football is fun
Football is wicked.

Sam Cottell (7)
Widcombe CE Junior School

THE MILLENNIUM BUG

The Millennium Bug,
Silence falls,
Computers crash,
Lights start dimming.

Candle light appears,
Electric flashes,
No heat, no electric,
Surrounded by darkness.

Rebecca Stone (8)
Wiveliscombe CP School

IN THE FUTURE

In the future will they reach Mars?
Who knows.
In the future will there be cars?
Who knows.
In the future will there be hover cars?
Who knows.
In the future will the sun go out?
Who knows.
In the future will the years pass?
Who knows.
In the future will I be alive?
Who knows.
In the future what will happen to computers?
Who knows.
In the future the Millennium Bug brings the world to a halt?
Who knows?

Matthew Cooper (8)
Wiveliscombe CP School

CELEBRATION 2000

The year 2000 is nearly here.
It's time to forget all you fear,
If you want to have some fun,
Well, it's just begun.
Think of no more shillings,
No more horses and carts,
No more canes, but more laughs,
All the pop music from Beatles to Steps,
All those hundreds of years we can't forget,
So let's give lots of cheers!

Lily Dove (9)
Wiveliscombe CP School

MEMORIES OH MEMORIES

Memories, oh memories

A thousand years will pass
Sad and happy things will happen

World War One is the saddest thing
Heroic men buried under poppies

First we had shillings
Now we have Euros

Memories, oh memories
What will the future hold

We've had a boost in inventions
We've even been to the moon and Mars

Electric is a giant thing
It's in nearly every home

Solar powered cars

Memories, oh memories,
What will the future hold

David Bowman (8)
Wiveliscombe CP School

THE MILLENNIUM BUG

Uh-oh, the Millennium Bug!
The Millennium Bug is coming!
Computers will die down.
Uh-oh, the Millennium Bug.

Computer experts
phoning round the town.
Shouting frantically, 'Buy this, buy that,
before it all goes wrong!'

Lights will fade.
Everyone's worried.
The Millennium Bug is scaring.
The Millennium Bug is daring!

Uh-oh, the Millennium Bug!
The Millennium Bug is coming!
Computers will die down.
Uh-oh, the Millennium Bug!

Sophie Hewitt (9)
Wiveliscombe CP School

INVENTIONS IN THE LAST HUNDRED YEARS

In the last hundred years,
People have made,
Computers, TVs
And roller blades.

In the last hundred years,
People made these things,
Pens and pencils
And drawing pins.

In the last hundred years,
People have made,
Paper and videos,
Buckets and spades.

In the next hundred years,
People will invent,
Lots of other things,
That nobody's dreamt.

Claire Coombes (9)
Wiveliscombe CP School

THE MILLENNIUM BUG

Are we going to lose the picture on our TV's?
We will have to wait and see.
Will we lose all track of time
Or will everything be fine?
Will al the computers go out
Or will all the people scream and shout?
Will the weather be affected
And all the fridges disconnected?
What will happen to all the cars?
Will we get a visit from planet Mars?
Will we be able to use our favourite mugs?
It all depends on the Millennium Bug!

Andrew Disney (9)
Wiveliscombe CP School

MILLENNIUM BUG

Sick bug stops our play,
The bus in the garden eat away,
The Millennium Bug no one knows,
Except the computer experts
Whose fear of this bug grows and grows,
They try to find an answer to stop it going amiss,
Because if they don't, it could bring and end to our earthly bliss,
So away with the Millennium Bug,
We don't want it here to stay,
We welcome the year 2000,
And hope it's a bug-free day!

Rebekah Thompson (8)
Wiveliscombe CP School

MILLENNIUM 2000

We don't know what's going to happen,
In the next one hundred years.
We might be working by lantern,
But it is coming near.

From penny-farthing to mountain bike,
Stewed up leaves to tea,
Inventions that we really like,
And will there still be trees?

We might be living in space,
In the next one hundred years,
Will we see an alien's face
In the next one hundred years?
Nobody knows!

Stephanie Valuks (8)
Wiveliscombe CP School

WHAT'S CHANGED 1900 - 2000

From Queen Victoria to Queen Elizabeth II,
Queen Victoria brought us enterprise and homes.
Queen Elizabeth brought us exercise and a Millennium Dome,
From books to TVs,
Books brought us craziness and laughter,
TVs have brought us sorrowfulness and heroics,
From World War I brought us blessedness and cheerlessness,
To World War II brought us earthworks and Spitfires.

Ashley Beale (9)
Wiveliscombe CP School

THE MILLENNIUM BUG

The millennium's here,
It's a brilliant New Year
When everyone's having fun,
We give a gigantic cheer,
For a fantastic New Year.

The lights will fade
When the Millennium Bug scares,
The computers will die out,
When the Millennium Bug dares
The radios will break down
When the Millennium Bug is near.

The millennium is here
It's a brilliant New Year
When everyone's having fun
We give a gigantic cheer
For a fantastic New Year.

What will we do without any lights?
What will we do without a computer?
What will we do without any radios?
What will we do?
When the Millennium Bug's near?

Kimberley Southcott (8)
Wiveliscombe CP School

HORROR!

The giants yell and blare once more,
The sound of thumping on the floor,
The lions roar, the snakes slither,
You see a witch start to wither.

The earth is burning in your hands,
In the front, an alien stands,
As the small creatures start to crawl,
The cauldron's boiling in the hall.

The deathly white ghosts haunt your home,
While the bad witches start to moan,
The beating and thumps in your heart,
That dreadful night before school starts.

Nathan Green (11)
Woolavington CP School

THE LEGGY LIZARD

Rushing in and out of rocks,
Chewing up caravan's socks,
Dashing down the sandy road,
Climbing on the back of a toad,
Jumping up caravan steps,
This little lizard is full of pep,
Wriggling through microscopic holes,
Scaring one million moles.

Michaelia Wheeler (10)
Woolavington CP School

THE WRITER OF THIS POEM

The writer of this poem
Is tall as a house,
As smooth as skin,
As thick as a mouse.

As quick as a flash,
As nice as my banner,
As cool as Sam,
As clumsy as Anna.

As runny as jam,
As strong as the wind,
As clean as the king,
As clever as Miss Barton.

Joanne Smith (10)
Woolavington CP School

A CAT

A loud purrer,
      A mouse eater,
A fast runner,
      A tree climber,
A paw-print maker,
      A floor scratcher,
A day sleeper,
      A bird leaper,
A four-footed lander.

Holly Aimson (11)
Woolavington CP School

THE WRITER OF THIS POEM

The writer of this poem
Is as smart as a dog,
As cool as a kid,
As long as a log.

As keen as you,
As sharp as a head,
As strong as a pencil,
As reliable as a bed.

As lazy as can be,
As bold as brass,
As tricky as a pin,
As green as grass.

The writer of this poem
Is not really true,
The writer of this poem
Is staring at you.

Anna Keegan (10)
Woolavington CP School

EAGLE

I fly,
Ever so high,
As free as the wind,
Higher than an aeroplane,
So high,
I fly.

Joe Blasby (10)
Woolavington CP School